The Future of Revolution

Jasper Bernes lives in Oakland and teaches in the English Department at the University of California, Berkeley. A regular contributor to the Field Notes section of the *Brooklyn Rail*, he is the author of *The Work of Art in the Age of Deindustrialization* and two books of poetry, *We Are Nothing and So Can You* and *Starsdown*.

The Future of Revolution

Communist Prospects from the Paris Commune to the George Floyd Uprising

Jasper Bernes

London • New York

This edition first published by Verso 2026
First published by Verso 2025

The manufacturer's authorized representative in the EU for product safety (GPSR) is LOGOS EUROPE, 9 rue Nicolas Poussin, 17000, La Rochelle, France
contact@logoseurope.eu

1 3 5 7 9 10 8 6 4 2

Verso
UK: 6 Meard Street, London W1F 0EG
US: 207 East 32nd Street, New York, NY 10016
versobooks.com

Verso is the imprint of New Left Books

ISBN-13: 978-1-78873-754-8
ISBN-13: 978-1-78873-755-5 (UK EBK)
ISBN-13: 978-1-78873-756-2 (US EBK)

British Library Cataloguing in Publication Data
A catalogue record for this book is available from the British Library

The Library of Congress Has Cataloged the Hardcover Edition as Follows:

Names: Bernes, Jasper, 1974- author.
Title: The future of revolution : communist prospects from the Paris Commune to the George Floyd uprising / Jasper Bernes.
Description: London ; New York : Verso, 2025. | Includes bibliographical references and index.
Identifiers: LCCN 2024051779 (print) | LCCN 2024051780 (ebook) | ISBN 9781788737531 (hardback) | ISBN 9781788737562 (ebook)
Subjects: LCSH: Communism—History. | Communism—Forecasting. | Communism and society. | Social conflict.
Classification: LCC HX45 .B474 2025 (print) | LCC HX45 (ebook) | DDC 320.53/2—dc23/eng/20241231
LC record available at https://lccn.loc.gov/2024051779
LC ebook record available at https://lccn.loc.gov/2024051780

Typeset in Minion Pro by MJ&N Gavan, Truro, Cornwall
Printed and bound by CPI Group (UK) Ltd, Croydon CR0 4YY

Contents

Introduction: Revolution and Its Examples

Marx tells us revolutions dress themselves up in the costumes of the past in order to speak the poetry of the future. But what in the history of communism since Marx's death is really new?

The powerful but now defeated communist movement of the twentieth century mostly rearranged nineteenth-century ideas and forms, Marxism among them. The party, the union, the commune; the uprising, the insurrection, the revolution; the strike, sabotage, seizure; anarchism, socialism, communism—all of this is from the nineteenth century. What is new is only the workers' council, the soviet, born in 1905 in Russia from the fires of the mass strike. Everything else has been more or less invariant since the late nineteenth century. In the twenty-first century, these old and sometimes forgotten ideas return in the guise of the new. And yet the poetry of the future is out there, ready to be spoken from behind the masks of the past, which persist as various fossilized radical ideologies. What this will look like we cannot say directly—it must be done before it can be thought. We can, however, trace out what will have needed to be done, and for this purpose it can be useful to study past revolutionary futures, those ideas of communism specific to past revolutions.

~

What follows is a long history of the workers' council as idea—long because it includes both its prehistory in the nineteenth century and its afterlife in our era. The workers' council is what I call a revolutionary example. The revolutionary example is an idea embedded in practice, an idea with a future, an idea that promises, through its own generalization, to usher in communism. It is action which, as example, as idea, finds its meaning in further action, in extension, intensification, and self-reflexive refinement, convoking the vast proletarian majority to participate in the abolition of class society and the establishment of classless human community.

I owe a large part of my fundamental approach here to others. I have little to add that is truly new but rather offer a fresh clarification of old debates and histories in the light of new ones. At the core of this study is a reading of a series of key communist documents: by Marx, Rosa Luxemburg, C. L. R. James, and many others. But my focus lies on the relevance of these texts to the present. For over a decade now, my engagement with struggles, directly or theoretically, has been influenced by the theory of communization, developed in France immediately after and in response to the failures of May '68. Communization emerges as a potent critique of what Gilles Dauvé, a seminal figure in the development of the theory, calls "the ultraleft," a constellation in which council communism looms particularly large. Communization is an internal critique of the concept of the council by true believers who found it lacking in the face of what May '68 revealed and the decade of struggle in the 1970s confirmed—a new era of class recuperation, economic stagnation, and crisis, in which labor could no longer affirm itself as a pole opposite to capital, and therefore could no longer posit the emergence of a revolutionary council system from the mass strike.

But this criticism of the ultraleft owes much to the ultraleft itself, and still retains certain core presuppositions from its interlocutors. Fifty years later, the differences between the 1960s council communists and their 1970s critics appear less stark. I am influenced in this view by one text in particular, an essay by a New Institute for Social Research, "Theses on the Council Concept," which defines the history of the council concept in such a way that we see what it shares with any communism which posits proletarian self-organization as its condition of emergence. For these writers, the council concept is "*essentially self-reflexive responsivity to natural and social conditions in the process of their collective transformation by individuals*" (italics in original).[1] Defined this way, "council" is a name for a series of functions that will need to be fulfilled by some social process or another if communist revolution is to succeed. "Council" then names, abstractly, fundamental aspects of the revolutionary example, as process that through its replication produces communism and through its self-reflexivity preserves and extends it. This self-reflexivity is a fundamental characteristic of any example that might serve to reproduce communism, whether commune or council, for it is a requirement of freely associated humans producing a life in common, a requirement of communism as it has been defined by proletarian struggle since at least 1848.

In this work, I distinguish what is eternal in the workers' council from what is historical. The history of communist revolution might be thought as a sequence of greater and lesser failures in which the logical contours of communist revolution become progressively sharper. The workers' council is a self-conscious refinement of the revolutionary example posited by the Paris Commune of 1871, which, despite its perhaps inevitable failure, provided for the world a new idea of the path to communism strong enough to cause Marx and many others to revise prior conceptions which emphasized the conquest and instrumentalization of state power. The Commune clarified for Marx aspects of communist revolution that would remain true—such as the necessity of the destruction of the armed power of the state and the arming of the workers. This Marx and many other nineteenth-century communists already knew, as such were the lessons of 1848. But the events of 1871 added for Marx a new restriction. When Marx writes that the Commune revealed that "the working-class cannot simply lay hold of the ready-made State machinery, and wield it for its own purposes," he discloses something that is forevermore true and likely always was true (on this last point Marx is equivocal).[2] As we will see, the council form is an elaboration and refinement of the commune

1 A New Institute for Social Research, "Theses on the Council Concept," 2019, isr.press.

2 Karl Marx and Friedrich Engels, *Collected Works*, vol. 22 (London: Lawrence & Wishart, 1988), 328.

form, adding further restrictions and revealing new requirements for communism.

Since the 1840s, Marx, both alone and together with Engels, had emphasized that class struggle itself would provide the theory by which class struggle was guided. "Communism is for us not a *state of affairs* which is to be established," Marx and Engels write in *The German Ideology*, "an ideal to which reality will have to adjust itself. We call communism the real movement that abolishes the present state of things. The conditions of this movement result from the premises now in existence."[3] This is perhaps their most important contribution to the theory of communism, a Copernican inversion of the moral, ideological, and sometimes religious strains of communist theory they encountered in the 1840s, demonstrating that the planets of the movement of communist intellectuals, with their competing ideas, orbit the sun of the proletarian movement. This is the very essence of their materialism, which roots ideas in social practice.

As something that emerges from struggle against capitalism, communism is in this sense always both idea and practice—it is an idea about practice suggested by practice itself. Following Gilles Dauvé, we can name the real movement of communism—that is to say, communist practice—the communist movement. But the communist movement is something other than a movement of communists, which is by and large an organization of the idea of communism. The communist movement rears its hydra heads only in specific revolutionary conjunctures, when particular forms of practice, whether commune, council, or something else, open up a path toward a communist horizon, a communist prospect, visible from some point of rising action. The movement of communists, however, exists as the anticipation or memory of communist movement. In nonrevolutionary moments, such as ours, the movement of communists becomes increasingly a guess or a wish, based on the memories of what happened the time previous and assumptions about what will happen next time, and therefore runs the risk of misalignment with communist movement when it reappears. As Dauvé notes, however, in revolutionary conjunctures a relay opens between communist

3 Karl Marx and Friedrich Engels, *Collected Works*, vol. 5 (London: Lawrence & Wishart, 2010), 49.

practice and communist ideas which partially absorbs the movement of communists into the communist movement, forcing it to contend with the facts of communist practice and class struggle more broadly.[4]

Perhaps the best example of this misalignment and its partial correction is the theory of the Second International—Marxism in the era immediately after Marx—as it collided with World War I and the consequent world revolution of 1917–23. This misalignment, however, persisted throughout the twentieth century, long after the Second International was destroyed by its own contradictions. A key registration of this misalignment in the face of the communist movement can be found in Rosa Luxemburg's seminal essay on the 1905 Russian Revolution, "The Mass Strike," which argued for the inadequacy of regnant social-democratic ideology when confronted with newly explosive forms of mass class struggle.[5] Unlike her anarchist contemporaries and Lev Trotsky, however, Luxemburg took no special notice of the soviets, the new workers' councils, whose example would soon span the world, indistinguishable in her account from the unions. She was thus not able to fully separate what was new in this moment from what was old.

Clarity about such matters would have to wait for the world revolution of 1917–23, when soviets and councils formed on a grand scale—in Russia, in Germany, in Italy, in Hungary, and as far afield as the United States and Norway. The shape, activity, and outcome of these councils were incredibly diverse, so diverse that no existing comparative historical study has really reckoned with their full sweep, the extent of their success, and the depth of their failure. I cannot do so here, in this slender study. What I can do is explore the idea of communism which these councils proposed, and those strains of the movement of communists which attempted to clarify, refine, and promote that idea of communism.

These strains would have little reach or influence during the interwar period. Inasmuch as so-called council communists had a limited

4 Gilles Dauvé and François Martin, *Eclipse and Re-emergence of the Communist Movement* (Oakland: PM Press, 2015), 110.

5 Rosa Luxemburg, *The Complete Works of Rosa Luxemburg*, vol. 4, *Political Writings 2: On Revolution (1906–1909)*, ed. Peter Hudis and Sandra Rein (New York: Verso, 2022), 193–262.

idea of the role of the party, were entirely critical of unions, and opposed any notion of popular front, they were entirely eclipsed by Leninism as it came to be formulated during the 1920s and 1930s. In the 1940s and 1950s, as the fraud of Stalinism and the triumph of world capitalism became clear, interest in this history and its adherents and exponents renewed. In the US, France, and Italy, small groups began to refocus communist theory on proletarian self-organization. Significant to this council communist survival and revival was the unique and, in many respects, sui generis theory and practice of C. L. R. James and Raya Dunayevskaya's Johnson-Forest Tendency, dissidents from the Trotskyist International who developed important ideas about the relationship between communist organization and proletarian self-organization. James and his colleagues introduced novel themes into the broader council communist revival, themes which would exert a strong influence, as told in what follows.

The Hungarian Revolution of 1956, which featured the re-emergence of workers' councils, galvanized this anti-Bolshevik current, but it was not until the 1960s that it would find real adherents. May '68 in France and the Hot Autumn in Italy generated dozens of new groups interested in the history of the workers' council that also had affiliates within the US and German New Left. To a real degree, our understanding of the history of the workers' council and council communism is formed retrospectively during this period. The biography of Paul Mattick is instructive here: a very young man during the German Revolution, Mattick participated in the council movement and the German Communist Workers' Party (KAPD), fleeing Germany for the US in 1926. During the years of the Great Depression, he put together a small council communist group in Chicago—the only organization of its kind in the US—and published important work in *International Council Correspondence* (an English-language affiliate of the Dutch-German *Rätekorrespondenz*) and *Living Marxism,* but increasingly in the 1940s and '50s he struggled to find publishers for his important, incisive writings, shut out by the mavens of the *Partisan Review* and the Institute for Social Research alike. It was only with the coming of the New Left and the revival of interest in the workers' council, first in Germany and then in the US, France, and Italy, that his important work finally found readers, and most of his publications date from the last two decades of his life.

A key amplifier within this revival was the theory and practice of the Situationist International, which placed the workers' council at the center of its unique blend of Marxism, anarchism, and avant-garde art, and which exerted an influence upon the intellectual output of the May '68 uprising far in excess of its real effect on the movement, and especially so when it came to the reception of French events by radicals elsewhere. Though no real workers' councils were formed in 1968, new council communists had good reason to expect that this was the way history would go, given the hostility of radical workers to the leftist parties and unions. Proletarian self-organization was again the motor of history, as events in France, Italy, the US, and China seemed to confirm. In the late 1970s, too, workers' councils formed in the Portuguese and Iranian Revolutions, in Chile during the Allende government, and in Poland. But these were for the most part not revolutionary or communist but organs of workers' self-defense. This was also true of the base organizations, workers' committees, and rank-and-file organizations formed in Italy during the Hot Autumn and after.

It is also true of self-organization during our own period, which often takes place without any revolutionary horizon, promising nothing so much as the reproduction of the proletariat as proletariat. We remain within the long shadow of 1968—not because of some imperious legacy of intellectual influence but because those events revealed a new structuring of class elements now nearly universal—visible in struggles from Hong Kong to Haiti, from Lebanon to Sudan. As the rate of growth of capitalism has slowed, so, too, has its ability to deliver meaningful pro-working-class reform, with a consequent withering of the institutions of the workers' movement, now vestigial forms of identification. In the past, proletarian self-organization took place against those institutions, positing revolutionary immediacy; increasingly, self-organization must make do in their place, employing insurrectionary means for fundamentally defensive aims. But struggles which have as their end the reproduction of the proletariat qua proletariat render "class belonging as external constraint," in the words of *Théorie Communiste*, and throw into question the ends of such movements in general, which can lead to a refusal of all negotiation or resolution as much as an indifference to it. Often these movements tend to posit self-reflexive ends, where the goal of struggle is struggle itself, without anyone knowing where it might lead, much less how it might lead there.[6]

Here one specific aspect of the grammar of 1968 looms large—the occupation outside the space of production. These are councils without workers, self-organized bodies that aspire to render the political and economic realities of late capitalism tractable but control nothing by which they might do so, inasmuch as they are constituted outside the spaces of production. Often their work is practical in focus, oriented toward material reproduction of the movement itself. Where they are deliberative, where they become assembly, they are often negatively deliberative, preventing consensus, sometimes to the point of refusing assembly altogether, such that focus is on practical matters entirely.

It is by now commonplace to suggest that this state of affairs—the death of the workers' movement and its institutions—means that we will need to start again at the beginning, to rebuild the parties and unions which once promised to lead the working class to salvation. But the twenty-first century is nothing like the nineteenth, and the conditions under which these institutions flourished—rapid industrialization, urbanization, proletarianization—obtain only in a shrinking portion of the world, and even there with important differences. Instead of beginning at the beginning, twenty-first-century communism will have to begin at the end, to truly start again, with new forms of organization and self-organization adequate to a stagnating capitalism, in which proletarian movements will find no allies among liberal or nationalist modernizers. What those forms of organization will look like we cannot say, but we can perhaps say something about what they will not look like, as well as the fundamental tasks they need to achieve. We can look to the communist movement of the past for an understanding of the logical structure of communism, what would have needed to happen, if only to understand better what will need to happen in the future.

---

6 Roland Simon, "The Present Moment," *Sic* 1, no. 1 (November 2011): 96, sicjournal.org.

Such reflection is, in fact, at the heart of the transformation of the practice of the workers' councils as it became the theory of council communism. A key figure here is Jan Appel, a participant in the German councils of 1918 and a founding member of the KAPD, created in 1920 in a large split from the German Communist Party (KPD), which declared that "the idea of the councils in the period of proletarian struggle for political power is at the centre of the revolutionary process."[7] By 1920 the councils of 1918 had been politically neutered, absorbed in many places by the trade unions or subordinated to social-democratic leadership. The KAPD and others within the broader council movement sought to revitalize these councils and make them the basis for a recommencement of the stalled social revolution. Appel's speech on behalf of the KAPD to the 1921 meeting of the Communist International, which expelled the group for its putative adventurism, puts forward a new idea of the relation between organized communists and the self-organization of proletarians, where the party is amplifier and catalyst, promoting struggles and ultimately aiming to transform them into a conciliar dictatorship of the proletariat, a means by which proletarians themselves would lay claim to the entire productive apparatus, now organized toward production for common use, not profit. As catalyst, the party would disappear through this process, dissolving into the thoroughly proletarian and communist councils whose conquest it facilitated.

In 1920 and 1921, this was a theory of how communists could still win. But the KAPD withered as revolutionary prospects declined, and by the late 1920s the theory of the councils that its partisans continued to develop became a theory of the next revolution, not the present one. In prison for his activities, Appel began a serious study of Marx and from it and his own experiences developed a model for communist production and distribution by way of workers' councils. From premises in Marx and his own experience, Appel derives that "the most profound and intense contradiction in human society resides in the fact that, in the last analysis, the right of decision over

7 Kommunistische Arbeiter-Partei Deutschlands, "Programme of the Communist Workers Party of Germany (KAPD)," May 1920, available at marxists.org.

the conditions of production, over what and how much is produced and in what quantity, is taken away from the producers themselves and placed in the hands of highly centralised organs of power."[8] In Marx's *Capital* Appel finds not only a theory of the workings of capitalism but an implicit vision of communism as dispossession negated, as direct proletarian control over the conditions of production. Marx's *Capital* becomes, among other things, a test of communism, a logical theory of what communism must achieve.

Appel synthesizes his gleanings into a book, *Fundamental Principles of Communist Production and Distribution* (*Grundprinzipien kommunistischer Produktion und Verteilung*), co-authored with the Group of International Communists (GIK) and published in 1930.[9] As the council communist revival of the 1960s will reveal, these fundamentals may not, in fact, stand up to the test of communism, a conclusion that both adherents to and critics of council communism in the '60s will reach. For some who participated in the events of May '68 in France, agitating for the establishment of workers' councils from the occupied universities, these events revealed key flaws within the theory of workers' power through councils as then conceived. Inasmuch as councils emerge before the destruction of state power and the market, they become instruments for negotiation over the value of labor power. Furthermore, even revolutionary councils organized in a particular way might preserve key aspects of capitalism and therefore fail to abolish it. Central to distinguishing what would work and what wouldn't was the question of value in capitalism, where the absence or presence of self-valorizing value becomes a key test for capitalism. As we shall see, however, the negation of value is not itself a test for communism, since capitalism might be abolished without turning into classless, stateless, moneyless society.

This immanent critique of the theory of the workers' council will give rise to what is known as the theory of communization, developed by *Invariance, Troploin, Négation, Théorie Communiste*,

8 Jan Appel, "Memories," 1966, available at marxists.org. More information on Appel as well as links to the original Dutch transcript can be found at Antonie Pannekoek Archives, aaap.be.

9 Group of International Communists of Holland (GIK), *Fundamental Principles of Communist Production and Distribution*, trans. Mike Baker (London: Movement for Workers' Councils, 1990).

and other ultraleft communist groups. For these groups, communist revolution is an expansionary social process rather than the flourishing of a particular social form. They replace the nominal theory of the council communists—in which the council is the goal—with an adverbial theory of communism, in which communism is less a form than a process. Workers' councils linked by revocable mandated delegates and a common plan might retain the division of labor in capitalist society, not to mention the division between work and the rest of life. Capitalist infrastructure, shaped by competition and production for profit, cannot simply be managed differently but must be transformed through enchained communist measures, specifically communist acts that would institute moneyless, stateless, classless reproduction. These measures would tend to break down rather than reinforce the divisions between one enterprise and another, between workplace and community, and between the time of work and the time of life.

In the long view, however, this theory might be as much a critique of council communism as an extension of it, a further regrounding of the theory in the self-activity of the proletariat, since communization takes from council communism a rejection of any program from above, any conception of the party as leader, organizer, or educator of the masses, as well as a withering critique of those workers' institutions, such as unions, designed to represent workers as workers. For partisans both of the council and of communization, theory remains an outgrowth of practice. The ideas that matter are those that animate millions of people in struggle, as the idea of the council or commune once did. The theory of communization anticipates the emergence of such an idea of communism immanent to twenty-first-century struggle. The point is to pay critical attention to proletarian struggle, to listen to what it has to say and to criticize it on its own terms, to disclose what such struggles would need to learn in order to succeed. This is in fact the only way a group dedicated to such principles might persist, its only reason for continuing, as reflection, synthesis, and clarification of existing struggles.

The early theory of the workers' council was not in itself a reason for going on—it was a theory of how to win, developed for conditions in which winning still seemed possible. This is the real end of theory: to become practice. Theory emerges from practice and returns to it, newly attuned. The communist revolution must be, among other things, an enormous theoretical achievement, an inquiry into the social and technical conditions of capitalist reproduction undertaken in order to dismantle and transform those conditions into communism. It is a work of distributed planning through which the self-activity of millions must be coordinated, balancing what can be known and what can be done with what can't, transforming necessity into the basis for freedom. The communist revolution will be a grand inquiry that is also a grand appropriation.

To be a council communist when there are no workers' councils means to accept rather radical limits on one's own activity, even perhaps an uncertainty about councils themselves, or at least an uncertainty about what the term means. One can participate in struggles, learn from them, and report on them without thinking one might shape or organize them. "There is nothing more to organize," writes C. L. R. James in his *Notes on Dialectics*. "Organization as we have known it is at an end. The task is to abolish organization. The task today is to call for, to teach, to illustrate, to develop *spontaneity*. The proletariat will find its method of proletarian organization."[10] James writes this text in 1948, as part of his developing break with the Trotskyist movement, under whose auspices he and others organized as the Johnson-Forest Tendency. Though still nominally involved in the Trotskyist movement, James's *Notes* works its way, using Hegel's schema, to a theoretical recognition that "there was no further place in the labor movement for the party." His emphasis on the creative elaboration of proletarian self-activity leads him to suspend even the organizational form of soviets, or councils, preferring more open-ended conditional formulations, in which "every worker to a man administered the economy of the state" and as a result both party and state dissolve into dispersed proletarian self-activity.[11] By 1956, however, reconstituted with his Johnson-Forest comrades as the Correspondence Publishing Committee and Facing Reality, James would treat the workers' councils of the 1956 Hungarian Revolution as proof positive of his earlier oracular claims. His co-authored

10 C. L. R. James, *Notes on Dialectics: Hegel, Marx, Lenin, Motive* (London: Allison & Busby, 1980), 171.

11 Ibid., 176.

book *Facing Reality* describes workers' councils as the "political form which destroys the bureaucratic state power, substituting in its place a socialist democracy … embracing the whole of the working population, organized at the source of all power, the place of work, making all decisions in the shop or office."[12]

But when there are no workers' councils, and one must be open-minded about even the form such revolutionary self-activity can take, what can one do to "to call for, to teach, to illustrate, to develop *spontaneity*"? One answer was to produce texts like *The American Worker*, whose purpose was "to understand what the workers are thinking and doing while actually at work on the bench or on the line," in order to locate the basis for such self-activity.[13] As a model taken up by other defectors from socialist and communist orthodoxy—such as Socialisme ou Barbarie in France and the group around the journal *Quaderni Rossi* in Italy—texts like *The American Worker* became a reason for organization that groups committed to proletarian self-activity might pursue. Called workers' inquiry and co-research, these projects developed in ways quite different from *The American Worker*, based on a clearer understanding of the problems facing such an endeavor.[14] Understanding what workers are thinking can be useful to the project of catalyzing revolutionary self-activity only if the workers themselves are part of such a process of inquiry. If the problem was, as James put it in *Notes on Dialectics*, the supersession of the antinomy between "the party as knowing," movement of communists, and "the proletariat as being," communist movement, then knowing must be the knowing of revolutionary proletarians in the act of abolishing themselves.

This makes the idea of *correspondence*, visible in the name that the James group took, Correspondence Publishing Committee, central to activity in non-revolutionary moments. Correspondence is a form of organization linking militant inquiry with proletarian

---

12 C. L. R. James, Grace Lee Boggs, and Cornelius Castoriadis, *Facing Reality* (Queens, NY: Factory School, 2006), 12.

13 Paul Romano and Ria Stone, *The American Worker* (Detroit: Bewick, 1972 [1947]), 10.

14 The notion of workers' inquiry can be traced to Marx's 1880 "Enquête ouvrière" published in *La revue socialiste*. Karl Marx and Friedrich Engels, *Collected Works*, vol. 24 (London: Lawrence & Wishart, 1994), 328–34.

struggle, making the latter an outgrowth of the former.[15] For some groups important to the council communist revival, correspondence becomes a form of anti-vanguardist organization, a set of linkages and exchanges between proletarians in struggle that might become the basis for actualized self-organization, a moment in the transformation of proletarian self-consciousness into self-activity. The group which splits from Socialisme ou Barbarie, centering the workers' council as an instrument of revolutionary proletarian organization takes the name Informations et Correspondances Ouvrières (ICO), acting as a clearinghouse for the exchange of reports and analysis by proletarians involved in workplace struggles but never intervening formally, as a group, in those struggles, insisting on the tactical and strategic autonomy of workplace committees and organizations. While ICO's version of council communism is a central object of critique for the post-'68 groups who develop the theory of communization, it is seen as symptomatic of the malady afflicting a far broader range of "ultraleft" groups. This is a critique of the ultraleft from within—however, one that never manages to constitute a real separation from it, insofar as it is only the ultraleft itself who might hear. What unites all these groups deriving from the council communist revival and its critique is the theme of inquiry as reason for being, a theme ultimately derived from the James group, as answer to the question of what an anti-party formation of communists might do in decidedly non-revolutionary moments, aside from participation in struggles as individuals. The best communist theory of the twenty-first century has been produced by such groups—from *Endnotes* to *Chuang* to *Angry Workers* to *Théorie Communiste* to the Field Notes section of the *Brooklyn Rail*, to name just a few publications—typically taking the form of inquiry into proletarian struggle, critical synthesis, and reflection on twenty-first-century uprisings. These forms of inquiry remain removed from the struggles themselves however, rejoining them in trickles not in torrents.

---

15 Like "inquiry," the term "correspondence" can be traced to Marx and Engels. The name of the first organization which the pair formed in Brussels in 1846 was Communist Correspondence Committee. The council communists also use the term for publications: *Internationale Rätekorrespondenz* in German (1934–37) and the corresponding English-language publication *International Council Correspondence* (1934–43).

Absent a revolution, the conditions for such a linkage of knowing and doing, movement of communists and communist movement, do not exist. It is only the emergence of proletarian self-activity that provides the conditions for an overcoming of the distinction between movement of communists and communist movement, as communist intellectuals join with and dissolve into proletarian self-activity or stand against it as obstacle. In non-revolutionary conjunctures, such an activity must remain spectral or speculative, or it must be simply a catalog of limits internal to proletarian action. What proletarians know in their everyday life is not necessarily what they know in conditions of collective action, since collective action involves learning; nor is it even what they would by definition need to know in revolutionary conditions for those conditions to be revolutionary. What matters for these moments is learning how to produce communism not learning how to live in capitalism. Inquiry into struggle is important for such a learning process, but this is also where everyday life becomes important as a repertoire of capacities, concrete skills for doing and making that revolution would proliferate and refine. Many of these skills are workplace skills, forms of knowledge inherent to the built environment, to the material infrastructure of capitalism, and therefore inherent in the project of dismantling and transforming that environment and material infrastructure.

Nonetheless these are lessons revolutions will have to learn. In his speech to the Comintern on behalf of the KAPD, Appel argues that communist militants must constitute a "framework" that the revolutionary proletariat can adopt as its own because it is "consistent with the development of the revolution to this point."[16] This involves the creation of factory groups, proto-councils, or workers' committees of communist militants, dedicated to the formation of revolutionary councils. In doing so, these factory groups provide an example of possibilities already present in struggle. Appel's *Grundprinzipien*, written after the factory groups had been destroyed, is also such an example, a working out in theory of an idea already present in the

16 John Riddell, ed., *To the Masses: Proceedings of the Third Congress of the Communist International, 1921*, Historical Materialism Book Series, vol. 91 (Leiden: Brill, 2015), 448–57.

councils of 1918. Today communication of such examples is the first task of communist revolutionaries—communists generalize tactics, such as blockades, occupations, and the use of lasers and fireworks against police, and place these tactics within particular strategic horizons. These are not simply examples but potentials, possibilities of struggle which need to be actualized in different contexts—that actualization is the theory generated by struggle.

I have divided this study into three sections. In the first, I tell the story of the workers' council as idea and as practice—that is, as revolutionary example—from the Paris Commune to the Spanish Civil War, reading key texts by Karl Marx, Rosa Luxemburg, Karl Korsch, Jan Appel, Amadeo Bordiga, and others, in light of revolutionary history. In the second, I examine Marx's mature theory of value as a "test of communism," an outline in negative of what communism would need to achieve to realize itself, and reflect on the proposals which council communists developed for the socialization of labor, as well as more recent debates these proposals have engendered. Many characters from the first section return as theoretical interlocutors in the second. In the third and final section, I examine the fate of the workers' council as idea and practice since World War II, when much of our understanding of the history of the workers' council and council communism was established but when the world seemed to transform in ways that called into question aspects of the council idea. Reading important texts by C. L. R. James, Guy Debord, Paul Mattick, Gilles Dauvé, *Théorie Communiste*, and others in light of the "long 1968," I trace the emergence of new ideas about the relationship between proletarian organization and theoretical inquiry, and end with an examination of these ideas in light of the George Floyd Uprising of 2020.

In developing this book I have found the collaboration and consultation of others indispensable. Writing of parts of this book was greatly helped by reading groups I held in 2022 and 2023, both online through the help of Red May and locally with Bay Area communists. This book can still be treated as a lecture—a reading of certain key texts. My conclusions here are preliminary, however, and readers are encouraged to examine the texts themselves and draw their own conclusions. For the most part, however, I have followed the conventions for historical writing rather than textual analysis and kept documentation to a minimum.

1

The Workers' Council and the Communist Prospect

Commune

We can speak of the Paris Commune of 1871 or the workers' councils of 1917–23 as ideas because these historical events reveal something logically true about class struggle. When Marx derives from the founding of the Paris Commune the fact that "the working class cannot simply lay hold of the ready-made state machinery, and wield it for its own purposes," he names something eternally true.[1] This transforms the Commune into an image of the future as much as a memory of the past. "The Commune," C. L. R. James writes, "showed the pattern of the future—to the millions and millions in the hundreds of thousands of cities who perhaps paid little attention to the Commune."[2] For James, writing in 1947, "Europe and Asia seethe[d] with would-be communards" because this historical

1 Karl Marx and Friedrich Engels, *Collected Works*, vol. 22 (London: Lawrence & Wishart, 1988), 328.

2 C. L. R. James, *Notes on Dialectics: Hegel, Marx, Lenin, Motive* (London: Allison & Busby, 1980), 77.

event revealed something axiomatic about class struggle and, for this reason, as James writes, "since 1917 the labor movement in country after country has repeatedly tried to imitate the Commune."

To imitate does not mean to repeat its failure but to take up where it left off, because just as much as the Commune comes from the future it also has a future—the Commune was a "thoroughly expansive political form," a germ of social organization which might have become the organizational structure not just of Paris but of France, Europe, and the world entire, "the political form at last discovered under which to work out the economic emancipation of labor."[3] This is a strong claim for Marx, but what positive characteristic of the Commune does it recommend? In what sense was this a discovery, and what precisely was discovered? What is the nature of commune as *political* form, rather than event, and to what extent can this be made the basis for the *economic* emancipation of labor?

Marx singles out several positive characteristics of communal constitution: First and foremost, the standing army was suppressed and replaced by the "armed people." Second, the Commune established a form of supervision from below, in which delegates elected by constitutive bodies are given explicit mandates, instantly recallable, and term limited—"responsible and revocable at short terms"—and thereby entirely subordinate to the whole of the working class through its base organizations.[4] Third, delegates receive no extra money for their administrative work, "done at workmen's wages" and simplified so that potentially any proletarian may participate.[5] Fourth, the communal administration was a working-class body and a working body, primarily constituted by workers and dedicated to their emancipation through specific measures and, ultimately, the establishment of a situation where "united cooperative societies are to regulate national production upon a common plan."[6] What is remarkable about Marx's predictive claim is that the soviets of 1905 and later of 1917–23 entirely vindicate it, inasmuch as they conform to all four conditions, at least aspirationally. Where soviets differ

3 Marx and Engels, *Collected Works*, vol. 22, 334.
4 Ibid., 331.
5 Ibid.
6 Ibid., 335.

from commune is in their specification of the fourth term—the councils are working-class and working bodies because, unlike the Commune, they are constituted in the workplace, the delegates workers themselves, and their primary task is the reproduction of communist society by production for need.

There is a contradiction, as I have already noted, between an emphasis on self-organization and a particular form of organization, unless one can demonstrate that some particular organization is a natural consequence of self-organization. It is one thing to argue that the working class must create its own forms of organization independent of the state and another to argue that some particular form *is* that organization. For Karl Korsch, writing in 1929, Marx's contradictory position on the Commune is reflected in later ambiguities that emerge from the council system, which Korsch sees as its direct outgrowth:

> When Marx celebrates this new commune as the finally discovered form for the liberation of labor, it was not at all his desire—as some of his followers later claimed and still do so to this day—to designate or brand *a definite form of political organization*, whether it is called a *revolutionary commune* or a *revolutionary council system*, as a singularly appropriate and potential form of the revolutionary proletarian class dictatorship. In the immediately preceding sentence, he expressly points to "the multifariousness of interpretations which supported the commune and the multiplicity of interests expressed in the commune," and he explained the already established character of this new form of government as a "*political form thoroughly capable of development*" ... The *revolutionary communal constitution* thus becomes under certain historical conditions the political form of a *process of development*, or to put it more clearly, of a *revolutionary action* where the basic essential goal is no longer to *preserve any one form of state rule*, or *even to create a newer "higher state-type,"* but rather to create at last the material conditions for the "withering away of every state altogether."[7]

7 Karl Korsch, *Karl Korsch: Revolutionary Theory*, ed. Douglas Kellner (Austin: University of Texas Press, 1977), 205–6.

This makes the fourth condition—the fact that the Commune was a working-class and working body, dedicated to the emancipation of workers through concrete measures—the most significant one: "its true secret was this: it was essentially a working class government." In Korsch's view, what mattered for the Commune and for the revolutionary council system was its proletarian, communist content not its form, where content here means not only *who* was organized by the Commune but *what* they did, with the answer being in the first case, proletarians, and in the second, emancipate themselves by abolishing class society. Content is a matter of composition but also function—the Commune was a form through which to "work out the economic emancipation of the proletariat."

Yet to function, the Commune needed to take form, to express itself in a definite set of relations, while remaining fundamentally working-class and communist in objective. While we might agree with Korsch that, where commune or council is concerned, its "true secret" is whom it comprises and what they do, we might nonetheless ask: Is the form simply indifferent, or is there something about the content which mandates certain forms? If proletarians themselves through the workplace are to produce according to common plan, thereby abolishing class, money, and the state, then we might deduce that delegation is a necessary though by no means sufficient condition of coordination, where coordination is a condition of universally distributed participation in planning. Everyone must be involved, and because everyone cannot meet in plenum, then there must be delegation. However, if it is to be proletarians themselves who economically emancipate themselves, then these delegates can only act expressly as the bearers of the direct intentions of their mass, proletarian electors; hence, they are responsible and recallable where these electors revoke their assent by asserting their fundamental control over the means of production, whether they do so explicitly or tacitly—that is, simply by refusing compliance. In other words, the structures of the commune can be deduced logically from more fundamental commitments—to self-organization of the proletariat, expropriation of the means of production, and production according to a common plan. But as logically deducible, then, these structures also derive from the common experience of class struggle. If the working class itself is to wrest the means of production from the capitalist class, these are the mechanisms that it must use and lessons that it must learn, whether from theory or from practice. This is why Marx described it as a form "at last discovered" and why the soviets of 1905 confirm these fundamental dimensions.

Because function and composition are what matters, as form the commune is "thoroughly expansive" (*ausdehnungsfähig*)—constructive, plastic, scalable. The flexibility of the form is directly connected to the fact that form itself is inadequate—a network of councils might revitalize the state, as Korsch notes, or reproduce capitalism, as its later critics note. But flexibility is also necessary if such a form is to spread, absorbing the vast majority of humanity. To absorb the proletariat entire and probably many others besides, such a form must be generalizable, adaptive. Its expansivity is spatial, geographic; it is a form fated to spread or die, to liberate all the world just as the value-form of capital has conquered all the world. But its expansivity is also dimensional, the commune is a self-similar, fractal form, with commune inside commune, communes of communes—designed to coordinate activity and disperse power. Finally, the commune does not expand contiguously—its spread has no borders and thus, as a form, it can leap from place to place, as it did from Lyon in 1870 to Paris in 1871. As an emblem of a universalizable capacity, this form capable-of-being-expanded "annexed to France working people all over the world" by providing an image of their future and of socialist possibility as such. In this sense, it is ethically expansive.[8]

The Paris Commune, then, was both "rallying cry and the thing itself," as Kristin Ross writes in *Communal Luxury*, her book on the afterlives of the Commune.[9] It was both a process and an event, both potentiality and actuality—it was potentiality as actuality, rallying cry as thing. The Commune was a fragment of some communism not yet established, a part without a whole, a potentially communist Paris that could actualize only by becoming the anti-capital of a communist France, Europe, and world. This explains its powerful resonance across space and time, explains James's assertion in 1947 that "Europe and Asia seethe with would-be communards."

---

8 Marx and Engels, *Collected Works*, vol. 22, 338.

9 Kristin Ross, *Communal Luxury: The Political Imaginary of the Paris Commune* (New York: Verso, 2015), 20.

Had it succeeded, however, would we still name it the Commune? We typically reserve the term for social experiments tragically out of place and time—Morelos, Berlin, Barcelona, Shanghai, Oakland. The appeal of such events comes from their embattled, isolated character. The desire to repeat, to declare the Commune here or there, is a desire to rectify, to transform the communal fragment into communist whole. As a thoroughly expansive form, a commune cannot find its content except by expanding, which perhaps explains why the practical measures adopted by the Commune were so disappointing, given its confinement to the Paris walls. Production for profit was not overcome within Paris by cooperative societies producing for common plan. Expropriations were limited to workplaces abandoned by their owners, and the cooperative economy, where wages could be equalized, was small, comprising only those workplaces under direct government control. Only the National Guard with its Central Committee operated according to revocable delegates, with general elections held to the Communal Council. The Labor Commission intended to set up federal structures of workers' control, but, outside of the National Guard, there was no direct way for base organizations to effect political decision, much less embark on a program of common production for communal need. Though the federally organized Women's Union comprised thousands of working women and was supported by the government, women were not allowed to vote in elections to the Communal Council. And although the Parisian working class was mobilized, armed and empowered through the National Guard, it is not clear that this was "essentially a working-class government," given how few pro-working-class actions were undertaken, though it's possible it could have been made into one.

Proletarian self-organization was nonetheless its primary mover if not its pilot. Unlike Blanqui's mechanical insurrection attempt of August 1870 in Lyon, organized conspiratorially, the rising of March 18 was a spontaneous reaction by the Parisian working class and poor to the French Army's attempt to disarm the Paris National Guard, forcing a wholesale retreat of the government from the capital. A newspaper of the Commune, printed the next day, described this as "a revolution without example in history … its fundamental greatness is that it is made entirely by the people as a collective communal revolutionary undertaking, anonymous, unanimous, and for the first time without leaders."[10] Proletarian self-organization is not necessarily revolutionary, but what made it so in this instance was that this spontaneous uprising dissipated the armed power of the state and replaced it with the central committee of the National Guard, comprising revocable delegates from the individual units. Inasmuch as this was an "essentially working-class government" it was because the workers were armed, formed into National Guard units controlled from below. The rising in Montmartre on March 18, however, included many women, not represented in the National Guard, and it is not clear how these units, democratic or not, could be the form whereby to work out the economic emancipation of the working class. Nonetheless, the first conditions of revolution—we can call these the conditions of insurrection—had been fulfilled: the smashing of the armed power of the state and the arming of the proletariat. This is the "true secret" which the Commune reveals, true for all time—without this, without the destruction of the army and the arming of the proletariat, there is no revolution.

But here self-organization encounters a limit. Proletarian self-organization is thoroughly expansive—it must expand or die. When limited to the walls of Paris and to the formation of armed power, the need for strategic unification and tactical centralization leads the democratic National Guard to become an army like any army. Only if the process of self-organization spread throughout the Parisian economy, into the countryside, and to other towns, to Lyon and Marseille and Toulouse, could such a state of affairs be avoided and a head-to-head clash with superior military forces averted. The universal appeal of the Commune's thoroughly expansive form cries out against such a state of affairs, calling allies to its side, encouraging a guerrilla struggle against capitalism without frontiers. As a fragment of communism, it represents actual hope to its contemporaries and future hope to its heirs. In this sense it is more than self-organization—for here the self-organization of a fraction means failure. As a rising of Paris demanding its autonomy, as an organization only of some section of the working class, it must fail. It is only by emblematizing possibilities for world communism, only

10 Taken from Donny Gluckstein, *The Paris Commune: A Revolution in Democracy* (Chicago: Haymarket, 2011), 5.

through its thoroughly expansive character, that it might succeed. The problem of the commune is the need for the other-organization of self-organization, for autonomy to realize itself in universality, for the proletarians themselves to organize according to a common plan, thereby abolishing themselves and all classes. In this sense the problem of the commune is the problem of the proletariat itself, a class that can emancipate itself only by abolishing itself as a class and all classes.

"Under the Commune Paris wanted to be not the capital of France but an autonomous collective in a universal federation of peoples," writes Kristin Ross in *Communal Luxury*, encapsulating the tension between autonomy and universality within the communal form.[11] The concept of the commune, she shows, developed during the Prussian siege as an idea of a "universal Republic," blending Proudhonian municipalism and Jacobin centralism. Many of its central figures were members of the International Workingmen's Association, a group explicitly dedicated to working-class internationalism, but whose French section, aligned with Bakunin, often supported autonomous proletarian action, such as the short-lived attempt to declare the Lyon Commune, which Marx and Engels thought foolhardy. Foreign members of the International assumed various leadership roles within the Commune, which effectively turned patriotic sentiment into anti-imperial sentiment opposed to both Bonaparte and the Prussians. As autonomous act, the Commune gained universal resonance, insofar as it projected a universalization of autonomy facilitated by production according to common plan.

The emancipation of the working classes must be, as we know from history and from Marx and Engels, achieved by the working class itself.[12] The class of proletarians must organize itself, must self-organize, for who else could be trusted to abolish class society and class rule but the class which cannot rule? In this sense, self-organization is presupposed by all meaningful class struggle, the prelude of insurrection if not revolution. But whose is the self of self-organization? What is the working class itself? It cannot be the sum

11 Ross, *Communal Luxury*, 12.

12 Karl Marx, "General Rules and Administrative Regulations of the International Working Men's Association," in Karl Marx and Friedrich Engels, *Collected Works*, vol. 23 (London: Lawrence & Wishart, 1988), 3.

of each worker as organized by capitalism, for that is by definition not self-organization but other-organization. Nor can it be the product of all workers organized for each other, for that is simply communism, leaving no room for another class and thus no room for classes or class as such. It must be the difference that some section of the class makes when it removes itself from its organization by capitalism and for the ruling class. Self-organization is always a matter of some section of the class that would be all but isn't. Self-organization is never, then, the class itself but some fraction of the class subtracted from given relations. To organize for themselves and by themselves, the members of some projective collectivity must do so with each other but most importantly against their already existing organization by and for capital. The proletariat steps forward by stepping back out of the existing organization of the world, but it never does so wholly. The proletariat is always only some proletarians.

Self-organization does not unite the working class, then, but splits it—in doing so, however, it betokens the abolition of class, not the unity of proletarians but real human community. Split upon split, self-organization inscribes the division between classes within the proletarian class in order that all divisions might be trespassed. Against a self-organizing fraction, the unity of the class presents itself as the subordination of each member of the class to their identity as exploited worker or dispossessed proletarian. The workers occupy their factories, but it is never all the workers or all the factories; nor, when a show of hands is taken, are the occupiers even the workers. Liberation means breaking with both the owners and the arbiters of labor power, breaking with the class of rulers as well as the class of the ruled, the owners and their delegates and representatives within the class, who enable the buying and selling of labor in bulk. But by the same measure, this exceptionality is also always a form of representation if not substitution. In self-organizing, such fractions are rarely entirely selfish in their motives, are rarely only strictly for themselves. This is why it is usually some moment of individual mournability that sets things off—the police kill a worker or some section of workers is fired, and then everyone reacts, for themselves and others all at once.

The workers occupy the factories in May '68, for example, but their demands are both selfish and not: they stand with the students, against De Gaulle, and for themselves. They inspire and are inspired by other proletarians near and far, with and without jobs, inside and outside any sociological boundary we might draw. The rebels of the Paris Commune, of the Shanghai Commune, of Berlin in 1918 and Bologna in 1977 and Argentina in 2001, act for themselves and others—not just Paris *or* Shanghai or Bologna or Buenos Aires or Cairo, but Paris *and* Shanghai and Bologna and Buenos Aires and Cairo. Inasmuch as they act in such a way as to make possible a later overcoming of class itself, then, they act on behalf of all proletarians, even and especially those not yet born into dispossession. In this manner, to the extent that they introduce something new into the class struggle, something imitable, they inspire sympathy, solidarity, and imitation far and wide.

As without, so within. The self of self-organization is spectral, dissolving at any moment into the frayed ends of individual selves. This is why all attempts to represent, to count, to fix the revolutionary camp in place, however defined, must fail. In collective action, people together believe what individually they doubt, making the boundaries of such actions indiscernible. Self-organization is a kind of fanatic reason—something is rational because in collective action people make it so. From the revolutionary red interval of 1917–23 through to the 1960s and 1970s, this is the conclusion we are led to draw from the shocking reversals and betrayals of the greatest revolutionary proletarian successes. In Germany in 1918, in the wake of the Russian Revolution, this dynamic was perhaps posed most clearly, if only because there the most massively inertial institution of the workers' movement, the SPD, confronted one of the largest fields of proletarian revolutionary self-organization yet seen. Communists like Rosa Luxemburg, organized with the Spartacus League and its successors, hoped to outmaneuver the left wing of capital by drawing upon the substantial support demonstrated by the workers' and soldiers' councils of November, spontaneous formations that had ended a world war and toppled the German empire. But in balloting, workers are counted modulo capital—as individual chunks of variable capital, heads of house, citizens, and consumers. A kind of Heisenbergian uncertainty attends self-organization then. Some subject, some specter, makes itself felt, makes its presence known, but cannot be represented or observed directly—and, in fact, it dissipates when one attempts to formalize or gather it, to body the ghost in constitution.

This is simply another way of saying that the object of self-organization is not, or cannot be, the securing of rights, for that is organization by and of another. Thus is the moment of contract, of settlement, always a scandal for struggles that insist on self-organization, whether *piqueteros* or Zapatistas, whether a *zone à défendre* or the Capitol Hill Autonomous Zone. Self-organization cannot become self-rule, cannot become a sovereign autonomy without becoming the domination of each individual by some abstract notion of the collective, some mediation, substitution, or representation. As atomized, penniless, and market-bound individuals, proletarians are weak, but collectivization is no guarantee against heteronomy, since capital treats labor as variable capital, bought in bundles that might be individuals or groups, a real-valued function that might as well be 1 worker or 1,000 workers or 12.57 workers, whatever that means. The collective action of a movement can be absorbed as a movement of variable capital, as a flow of labor power reproduced at a given capacity.

This explains the sudden reversals experienced when it comes time to settle up. In June of 1968 in Paris, the mass of workers greet the negotiations between the leaders of the respective classes with an indifference equal to the ferocity with which they downed their tools in the great strike of May. In Italy's Creeping May, the rank-and-file organizations which brought the apparatus of Italian industry to halt with ease dissipate just as quickly in the face of negotiations between the classes. The informality of self-organization cannot be banished, cannot be formalized, no matter the tyrannies imposed by such lack of structure. That lack of structure, or rather that refusal of structure, derives from the antinomies of the class struggle.

For this reason, even though self-organization is the very presupposition of revolutionary action, as and if the revolution unfolds it becomes an obstacle which the revolution must overcome.[13] Perhaps "limit" is the better term, for it is not what self-organization does that

13 Roland Simon, "L'auto-organisation est la premier acte de la revolution, la suite s'effectue contre elle," *Meeting* 3 (June 2006): 3–17.

hinders the revolution but what it doesn't do. The self-organizing fraction cannot wholly subtract itself, for it remains materially dependent—that way lies suicide. Nor can it simply transact or contract, for that would be organization by and through the enemy class. It must extract from capital and retract from the state what is necessary for each self to organize itself with others according to its own desire, which is to say nearly everything. The self of self-organization is projective, prospective—not the real individuals themselves but a kind of spirit that hovers near. It doesn't exist here and now, and therefore can look on itself strictly as itself—as worker in an auto plant, parent in a neighborhood, citizen in a city—as in fact the self of another, as something to be abolished. Self-organization always fights its way into a corner where the options are suicide, compromise, or total victory—which is to say, the overcoming of the opposition between self and other in the sense used here, the abolition of classes. Absent the production of communism, of classless society, such a self presents as vengeful spirit, and appears most clearly when destroying the things of this world.

1905 and the Mass Strike

As Korsch makes clear in his essay on the Commune, "the revolutionary ideas of the Paris communardes of 1871 are partly derived from the federalistic program of Bakunin and Proudhon, partly from the circle of ideas of the revolutionary Jacobins surviving in Blanquism, and only to a very small degree in *Marxism*."[14] There is thus for Korsch a major contradiction between Marx's unqualified endorsement of this form and the strongly centralist positions he took within the International, both before and after the Commune. For Korsch, Marx's advocacy was essentially a rhetorical maneuver, assimilating the federalism of the commune form to his own centralism as part of his debates with the anarchists within the First International:

14 Korsch, *Karl Korsch: Revolutionary Theory*, 207.

> For the sake of the revolutionary *essence* of the Paris Commune, he repressed the critique which from his standpoint he should have exercised on the special *form* of its historical manifestation. If beyond that he even went a step further and celebrated the political form of the revolutionary communal-constitution directly as the "finally discovered form" of the proletarian dictatorship, then the explanation does not lie any more merely with his natural *solidarity* with the revolutionary workers of Paris, but also in a special, *subsidiary purpose*. Having written the Address to the General Council of the I.W.A., directly after the glorious battle and defeat of the Paris communardes, Marx not only wanted to *annex the Marxism of the Commune but also at the same time the Commune to Marxism.*[15]

What would Marx's repressed critique be here? Presumably, Marx would emphasize the lack of any economic organization to the Commune, specific means whereby the workers themselves could produce for social need, their need, according to a common plan. It is this notion of plan which is partly foreign to the idea of the Commune, and essential to the positions which Marx and Engels were in the process of hegemonizing within the International. Unlike the Proudhonians, who thought these individuals might continue to transact through the market, and unlike Bakunin and his fellow collectivists, who thought that base collectives could freely and mutually transact from a starting point of absolute autonomy, Marx thought unitary economic organization the first condition of free association, rather than a contingent one. By making political rather than economic organizations primary, or rather, by failing to effectively overcome the distinction between the political and the economic, the Commune risked assimilation by the bourgeois state. The dangers of such formalism here are clear. As Korsch writes:

> As incorrect as it may be to see with Proudhon and Bakunin an overcoming of the bourgeois state in the "federative" form, it is just as incorrect when today some Marxist followers of the revolutionary commune on the revolutionary council system believe on the basis of

15 Ibid., 209.

> such misunderstood explanations by Marx, Engels, and Lenin that a parliamentary representative with a short-term, binding mandate revocable at any time, or a government functionary employed by private treaty for ordinary "wages," would be a less bourgeois arrangement than an elected parliamentarian.[16]

For Korsch, only the content of the Commune matters—this is what is essential, its revolutionary working-class character. Independent of such content, such function, there is nothing inherently revolutionary about the commune form—federation by way of revocable delegates might be the means for a purely bourgeois organization, since municipal communes date to the medieval struggles of the urban bourgeoisie against the landed nobility. Korsch is right as a matter of logic, and the later experience of the German Revolution, where the councils of 1918 were eventually incorporated into the Weimar constitution as "works councils" (*Betriebsräte*) that still exist today, proves him right by history. But rendering the commune form inadequate is one thing, rendering it irrelevant is another. It may be that the commune form is a necessary but not sufficient condition of revolution; in other words, it may be the case that wherever emancipation is conquered by the working classes themselves, this form or something like it will need to reappear, as it did in 1905, as it did in 1917, and as it perhaps should have in later revolutions, such as Spain in 1936.

This is the essential link between the commune and the councils, that which between them proletarians recognize as natural, as logical consequence of their struggle, a form that must be adopted for proletarian struggle to become revolutionary. Lev Trotsky, in his writing on the 1905 Russian Revolution and his participation in the St. Petersburg Soviet, makes these logical conditions clear. The soviets were a "response to an objective need … born of the course of events," the only way to rapidly massify the struggle through the organization of a political general strike with the broadest participation.[17] What were needed were organizations "*of the proletariat*" not merely "*within the proletariat*," as Trotsky and his fellow Social

---

16 Ibid., 210.

17 Leon Trotsky, *1905* (New York: Random House, 1971), 104.

Democrats, organized semi-clandestinely, were at the time.[18] As objective need, the soviet mediates between party and class for Trotsky. He describes the soviets as non-party expedients the party takes to broaden its support, but also as "natural organ of the proletariat in its immediate struggle for power as determined by the actual course of events," leading one to question the necessity of the party. In Trotsky's account the party initiated the soviet through a convocation of delegates, but the work to be done was the recognition of an already established unanimity.[19] The soviets were "an answer that came of its own accord" to questions the revolution posed.[20] As he writes, "Every step of the workers' representation was determined in advance. Its 'tactics' were obvious. The methods of struggle did not have to be discussed; there was hardly time to formulate them."[21]

As means, however, the soviets become ends. Within social democracy, the revolutionary general strike, as opposed to the limited political demonstration strike, was often thought a logical impossibility, inasmuch as workers would suffer the worst consequences of a global interruption of production, requiring them to engage in armed overthrow of the state. But if the workers were sufficiently powerful to do that—something influential figures of the era such as Engels thought impossible, given the development of repeating rifles and explosive ordnance—then the general strike was a needless intermediary step. The soviet, for Trotsky, solves this problem by taking up the organization of social functions precisely where they are paralyzed: "The more completely a strike renders the state organization obsolete, the more the organization of the strike itself is obliged to assume state functions. These conditions for a general strike as a proletarian method of struggle were, at the same time, the conditions for the immense significance of the Soviet of Workers' Deputies."[22] As such, the soviet becomes a "workers' government in embryo."[23]

18 Ibid., 251.
19 Ibid.
20 Ibid., 105.
21 Ibid., 106.
22 Ibid., 252.
23 Ibid., 251.

Like Marx's writings on the Commune, Trotsky's narrative of 1905 annexes the soviet to Marxism by establishing a natural leadership role for the party but at the same time acknowledges the essential revolutionary character of the non-party soviet, endorsing a form of revolutionary workplace organization with distinctly anarchist and syndicalist origins. The same might be said for Rosa Luxemburg's essay on the 1905 revolution, "The Mass Strike," which repositions the party with regard to proletarian self-activity, annexing to Marxism the anarchist and syndicalist theory of the general strike but at the same time setting sharp limits on the party's leadership. It does so, however, by treating the mass strike as a purely pre-revolutionary phenomenon. The term "mass strike" had been coined by Karl Kautsky in 1892 to distinguish social-democratic treatment of the question of generalized strikes from the anarchist and syndicalist theory of the general strike, but his use of the term refers to a singular event and not the unfolding process which Luxemburg describes. Luxemburg has two opponents in mind in this text, both of whom treat the mass or general strike as event rather than process—on the one hand, caricatured anarchists who imagine the strike as a unanimous, total, and irrevocable withdrawal of labor that brings state and economy to its knees; on the other, social democrats who imagine that the mass strike is simply a political implement, to be used judiciously by the party in the service of campaigns for reform. She writes:

> Both tendencies proceed on the common purely anarchistic assumption that the mass strike is a purely technical means of struggle which can be "decided" at their pleasure and strictly according to conscience, or "forbidden"—a kind of pocket-knife which can be kept in the pocket clasped "ready for any emergency," and according to the decision, can be unclasped and used.[24]

In opposing itself to a fundamentally Bakuninist and conspiratorial notion of the general strike, social democracy had taken as given that such strikes could be decided, and thus it transformed

---

24 Rosa Luxemburg, *The Complete Works of Rosa Luxemburg*, vol. 4, *Political Writings 2: On Revolution (1906–1909)*, ed. Peter Hudis and Sandra Rein (New York: Verso, 2022), 198.

discussion of the general strike into discussion of the practicability of the parties calling such a strike or assessment of general strike attempts by social democrats and syndicalist organizations organized in support of suffrage or the eight-hour workday, such as had occurred in Belgium and then Sweden in 1902. Against the anarchists and the antipolitical syndicalists the 1905 Russian Revolution showed the mass strike to be a phenomenon oriented toward political reforms such as suffrage and the eight-hour day, but against the social democrats these were not struggles that could be controlled or called for by party leaders.

As Trotsky saw the soviet, so Luxemburg saw the mass strike as "a historical phenomenon which, at a given moment, results from social conditions with historical inevitability."[25] It could not be organized in advance; one cannot "go house-to-house canvassing with this 'idea' in order to gradually win the working-class to it."[26] It simply appears, as living example, and finds adherents among those who would have called it foolish if only told about it. Throughout the text Luxemburg develops a theoretical vocabulary remarkably close to what will eventually be called complexity theory. The mass strike is what complexity theorists call an "emergent" phenomenon. Just as one cannot calculate the macroscopic behavior of a chaotic physical system from the microscopic behavior of its component particles, one cannot treat the mass strike as a consequence of individual acts of reason. "An artificially arranged demonstration of the urban proletariat, taking place once, a mere mass strike action arising out of discipline, and directed by the conductor's baton of a party executive, could therefore leave the broad masses of the people cold and indifferent," Luxemburg writes.[27] But unreasonable, even adventurist action might produce its own reasons after the fact, and "a powerful and reckless fighting action of the industrial proletariat, born of a revolutionary situation, must surely react upon the deeper-lying layers, and ultimately draw all those into a stormy general economic struggle who, in normal times, stand aside from the daily trade-union fight."[28] As such,

25 Ibid., 170.
26 Ibid., 171.
27 Ibid., 198.
28 Ibid.

> it is extremely difficult for any directing organ of the proletarian movement to foresee and to calculate which occasions and factors can lead to explosions and which cannot … because in every individual act of the struggle so very many important economic, political and social, general and local, material and psychical, factors react upon one another in such a way that no single act can be arranged and resolved as if it were a mathematical problem.[29]

Throughout the text Luxemburg compares the mass strike to turbulent natural phenomena, to a chaotic liquid (the adjective "stormy" is used thirteen times). The mass strike "flows now like a broad billow over the whole kingdom, and now divides into a gigantic network of narrow streams; now it bubbles forth from under the ground like a fresh spring and now is completely lost under the earth."[30] The behavior of such systems is chaotic, turbulent; they do not develop in a straight line. She offers this account of the mass strike as an alternative to that of Eduard Bernstein, whose *Evolutionary Socialism* repudiated any violent clash between capital and labor and instead saw class struggle as gradual evolutionary process—the general strike was, for Bernstein, a pacificist alternative to armed confrontation, useful in supporting parliamentary reform.[31] Like Bernstein, however, Luxemburg sees the mass strike chiefly as an organizing and developing force, not as something directly revolutionary. Her temporalization of the mass strike applies likewise to the revolution—the revolution is a process, not an event, one which might involve street fighting one day and struggles for reform of parliament the next. Though this development tends toward "general open insurrection," it does so through "preparatory partial insurrections" which widen the terrain of action by organizing the unorganized and drawing in those sections of the class not included within trade unions and parties.[32]

Yet there is nowhere in Luxemburg's text the sense that the executive structures of the mass strike might become a workers'

29 Ibid.

30 Ibid., 221.

31 Eduard Bernstein, *Evolutionary Socialism: A Criticism and Affirmation* (New York: Schocken Books, 1961).

32 Luxemburg, *The Complete Works of Rosa Luxemburg*, vol. 4, 190.

government, that the organization of the strike might become the organization of the revolution, as Trotsky describes. Indeed Luxemburg hardly singles out the soviets, except for a single mention of the campaign for the eight-hour workday, imposed by fiat by the St. Petersburg Soviet. Whereas Trotsky might see this as a workers' government in embryo, the soviet regulating wages directly, Luxemburg simply sees this as extension and massification of the struggle, workplace by workplace. The mass strike unfolds as a relay between political and economic actions, between centripetal, singular political events, such as the January massacre, the October general strike, and the December insurrection, and periods of centrifugal, dispersive economic actions at the enterprise level. Rather than a falling off, or depoliticization, as some social democrats feared, these centrifugal moments are an extension of the struggle, bringing in new layers. Alternating political intensification and economic extension work to deepen the struggle, wave upon wave, unto general insurrection. Luxemburg's distinction between economic and political struggle, however, works only insofar as one imagines a revolution, as in Russia, where the state and capital persist, and the party and trade unions with them. The form of the commune is, in Marx's characterization, the *political* form in which to work out "economical emancipation." Political decentralization becomes the precondition of unitary economic organization, abolishing the state as a sphere separate from social reproduction and thus abolishing all distinction between economic and political forms. The direct regulation of the workday, for example, by the St. Petersburg Soviet is neither economic nor political but both and neither—it can be effected, however, only inasmuch as it has really abolished capital and the state. Neither party nor trade union, the amphibian soviet is at once economic and political, and in this sense it is a "worker's government," otherwise a contradiction in terms.

Luxemburg will, a dozen years later, become an advocate of the soviet but an ambivalent one, especially where it concerns the distinction between economic and political struggle, and their institutional bearers, the trade unions and parties. Her Spartacus League, the germ of both the German Communist Party (KPD) and its majority successor, the German Communist Workers' Party (KAPD), will champion the workers' and soldiers' councils of November 1918, which end the world war and the German empire. In her essay "What Does the Spartacus League Want?" she advocates for the dispersive supervision-from-below of the commune, fusing it to the specifically workplace-based energies of the mass strike:

> From the uppermost summit of the state down to the tiniest parish, the proletarian mass must therefore replace the inherited organs of bourgeois class rule—the assemblies, parliaments, and city councils—with its own class organs—with workers' and soldiers' councils. It must occupy all the posts, supervise all functions, measure all official needs by the standard of its own class interests and the tasks of socialism. Only through constant, vital, reciprocal contact between the masses of the people and their organs, the workers' and soldiers' councils, can the activity of the people fill the state with a socialist spirit.
>
> The economic overturn, likewise, can be accomplished only if the process is carried out by proletarian mass action. The naked decrees of socialization by the highest revolutionary authorities are by themselves empty phrases. Only the working class, through its own activity, can make the word flesh. The workers can achieve control over production, and ultimately real power, by means of tenacious struggle with capital, hand-to-hand, in every shop, with direct mass pressure, with strikes and with the creation of its own permanent representative organs.[33]

Even here, though, Luxemburg retains a separation, in her paragraphs, between the economic and the political that the councils themselves should overcome. And in practice she will vacillate on the question of a hard break from the SPD and its affiliate trade unions, worrying that in this way she and her comrades might lose contact with the masses. The program outlined in her essay constitutes what might be called the "conciliar republic," picking up where her essay "The Mass Strike" left off and outlining what happens after the general insurrection to which the mass strike tends, how the workers might thereby emancipate themselves, now recognizing the centrality of the soviet form. Like the commune, the first act is "disarmament of the entire police force and of all officers and

33 Rosa Luxemburg, *The Rosa Luxemburg Reader* (New York: Monthly Review Press, 2004), 351.

nonproletarian soldiers," and its second and third "confiscation of all weapons and munitions stocks as well as armaments factories by workers' and soldiers' councils" with a subsequent "arming of the entire adult male proletarian population as a workers' militia."[34] As with the Paris National Guard, this militia is constituted by "voluntary discipline of the soldiers," its officers elected, and with no military justice system.[35] But rather than dissolving or abolishing the bourgeois state, Luxemburg's council republic would overgrow it, ensnaring it with its delegative vines and, not unlike Lenin's conception in *State and Revolution*, using its force to establish universal decree. "Elimination of all parliaments and municipal councils, and takeover of their functions by workers' and soldiers' councils, and of the latter's committees and organs" might, as Korsch warns, simply reproduce bourgeois function with a nominally proletarian form. Though parliament is eliminated in Luxemburg's program, there is still need for "radical social legislation" in this conciliar republic, shortening the working day to six hours. This is in part because bourgeois control over production is partly retained—this is a transitional document, socializing all "banks, mines, smelters, together with all large enterprises of industry and commerce" along with "the entire public transportation system," but in other enterprises private ownership would persist, constrained by the conciliar republic and the continuation of the mass strike, in advance of eventual socialization by workplace-based "enterprise councils."[36]

The Soviet

As both concept and actuality, the soviet emerges naturally from the spontaneous mass strike—the originating St. Petersburg Soviet is formed during the October 1905 general strike, a centripetal moment of politicization within the revolutionary year, though some accounts trace it back to the aftermath of Bloody Sunday in January. The soviet is, at first, an instrument for the generalization

34 Ibid., 354.
35 Ibid.
36 Ibid.

of the strike. In extending and intensifying the strike, it becomes expression of proletarian unanimity—a collective will to quiet and assert dominion over the machinery of production. It is this direct power over production that renders the soviet, potentially, "a political form … in which to work out the economic emancipation of labor." As coordinating body, the soviet not only enforces the strike but grants exceptions for vital services. In this sense its destiny is direct control over production by the workers themselves. Rather than merely petition for legal limits to the workday, the members of the St. Petersburg Soviet attempt to impose the eight-hour day themselves, challenging the authority of the state. In the wake of the October 1905 general strike, and the proclamation of new liberal freedoms by Nicholas II, the printers associated with the St. Petersburg Soviet directly circumvent censorship laws but also engage in their own censorship of right-wing literature calling for pogroms against the workers.

There is a big difference, however, between coordinating a strike or even an insurrection and coordinating the reproduction of communist society. In this sense the soviet is, like the commune, both rallying cry and thing itself. After 1905, as idea, the soviet could not be forgotten, but inasmuch as the soviet was an incipient form whose promise had not been realized, it could also not be remembered—its precise revolutionary function had to be discovered. In 1917, soviets return immediately, even before they could be elected from the workplaces. On February 27, members of the Menshevik Central Workers Group, freed from prison, formed the Temporary Executive Committee of the Soviet of Workers' Deputies in St. Petersburg and called for elections in the factories and barracks. Bigger factories were to select one delegate per 1,000 workers, whereas each enterprise smaller than 1,000 would send a single delegate. But this executive committee of party members never ceded control to the delegate body. Selecting representatives from each of the political parties, it would continue to make decisions independent of the delegates, sometimes submitting them for approval and sometimes not. Before the October Revolution, this was primarily a political body, leveling demands on the legislature and coordinating with unions and parties. It was not a mechanism of workers' control. And yet the idea of workers' control persisted, and everywhere factory committees formed, sometimes including delegates to the soviet, sometimes not. These committees would exert pressure on management, especially in the state sector, but also coordinate with each other to continue production where owners or managers had fled. There thus came to be a division between the soviet as political organ and the factory committee as economic organ. The soviets were not an organ through which the factory committees could exert power, and, in some cases, the factory committees attempted to create alternative soviet structures, a move that would be repeated in Germany in 1920.[37]

What is a soviet? Is it the name for the delegate body or the mass of electors? When Lenin declaims, following his return to Russia in April 1917, "all power to the soviets," to whom does this power devolve? In 1877, during a nationwide rail strike that had become insurrectionary in Baltimore and Pittsburgh, drawing in workers outside of the direct rail industry, some associates of Marx and Engels organized through the Workingmen's Party of the US took charge of the strike in the city of St. Louis, establishing an executive committee with delegates from the various unions, and enforcing a citywide general strike. The St. Louis elite, their antiworker imaginations stoked by lurid stories from France, referred to the strike as "the Commune" and, inasmuch as the executive committee issued dispensations for certain enterprises performing vital services to continue, in order that the strike not unduly harm the workers themselves, we might, following Trotsky's reasoning, see this as nascent workers' self-government. But this was a commune largely established from above, and easily folded up by the reactionary militias which city leaders formed in response to the strike. It was formed by delegates from existing workers' organizations, not direct elections by the workers themselves. It was not a soviet, in this sense, because there were no electing bodies, no workers' assemblies supervising it from below.

Likewise, the soviets of 1917 lacked any mechanisms of feedback, revocation, or mandate that might direct them from below. The factory committees attempted to create their own central councils, but this only reinforced the division between the economic and the

37 See Axel Weipert, *The Second Revolution: The Council Movement in Berlin 1919–20* (Leiden: Brill, 2023), 117–237.

political, and these councils were only nominally responsible to the factory committees—"all decrees of the factory committees were ultimately dependent on the sanctions of the Central Council, and the Council could abolish any decree of the factory committees."[38]

As instrument for the generalization of the mass strike, the workers' council is a double form, both intensive, filling the workplace with a plenary mass of strikers, and extensive, spreading from workplace to workplace. At first, as the strike moves toward insurrection, the soviet is the coordination of a unanimity—as Trotsky tells us in *1905*, there was nothing to be debated or discussed, only plans to be put into action. The soviet formalizes a unanimity of action and solidarity already present, renders it self-reflexive, a matter of will, of pledges. This coordination will already have been taking place, through ad hoc exchanges conducted by unions and parties, but the soviet formalizes both the intensive, plenary character of the mass strike and its extension across enterprises. The strike must be voluntarily unanimous and massive, it must represent the majority of workers, and it must be coordinated—revocable, mandated delegates meet these logical requirements. As organization of the workers' themselves, and as interruption to production, it is both economic and political at once.

Once the mass strike transforms into revolution—once the armed power of the state collapses—the tasks facing the councils transform. No longer the expression of a unanimous negation, the councils must socialize wealth and directly organize social reproduction. They must now become a unanimous affirmation of a common plan, voluntarily assented to by the freely associated councils, by way of revocable, mandated delegates. No workers' councils have successfully negotiated this transition—from instrument of the mass strike and insurrection to instrument of socialization. Inasmuch as "council communism" names a tendency within the global revolution of 1917–23, this is a tendency which aims to transform the spontaneously emerging councils of the mass strike and insurrection into instruments of common plan—that is to say, communism—directly assented to by the workers themselves. In Germany, where

38 Quoted in Peter Rachleff, "Soviets and Factory Committees in the Russian Revolution," *Radical America* 8, no. 6 (1974): 102.

this tendency was strongest, the councils were effectively neutered, transformed into political instruments, from the very first days of the revolution. The partisans of the council aimed to revitalize and refound the councils, electing new delegates directly from the workplaces and transforming them into explicitly communist and proletarian mechanisms.

As in Russia in 1917, the workers' councils of the 1918 German Revolution emerged directly from the antiwar mass strike movement of the German proletariat. From 1914 on, the SPD collaborated with the Kaiserreich to prohibit strikes and criminalize workers' organizations. As the war ground to a halt in 1916 and wartime rationing led to the immiseration of the working class, the Shop Stewards Movement, a clandestine network of shop-floor delegates within the wartime metal industry, led a mass illegal strike in April 1916, in response to the arrest of Karl Liebknecht, who had formed the antiwar Spartacus League in 1914 with Rosa Luxemburg and others. Though Luxemburg's 1906 polemic on the mass strike had succeeded in winning a nominal endorsement of the tactic by the party, these were in fact the first German mass strikes, now organized entirely outside of and in opposition to the party. The German state responded by further criminalizing workers' organizations and conscripting strike leaders such as machinist Richard Müller into military service, but the Shop Stewards network was designed to survive such repression through a system of alternates, and they organized another, even larger mass strike in April 1917. It was during this strike that workers' councils as instruments of the mass strike were formed, first in Leipzig and then in Berlin, no doubt inspired by the Russian example.

This history calls to mind the alternate origin story for the soviet, found in anarchist Voline's late-published account *The Unknown Revolution*.[39] According to Voline, the soviet did not emerge from the October mass strike, as Trotsky avers, but from the events of January. As is well-known, the march on the Winter Palace was organized through the Gapon union, an association the tsarist secret police had established to control the workers' movement. Outrage in response

39 Voline, *The Unknown Revolution, 1917–1921* (Montreal: Black Rose Books, 1975), 89–103.

to the firing of Gapon union members at the Putilov Iron Works led, despite the counter-revolutionary design of this union, to a mass strike and a march on the Winter Palace, culminating in the massacre that would set off the revolution. In Voline's account the soviet was formed directly after Bloody Sunday as a way for former members of the Gapon union to coordinate without police surveillance, just as the Shop Stewards established a semi-clandestine network of delegates to organize independently of the collaborationist trade unions.

The Shop Stewards organized another mass strike in January 1918, this time explicitly aimed at toppling the regime. The proto-conciliar structure of the Stewards Movement was formalized, with a network of 414 delegates representing over 400,000 workers. Despite the objections of the Spartacists, the Stewards called off this strike, anticipating a massacre if they pushed forward to insurrection. This failure, however, solidified the revolutionary objectives of the network and, as the German war effort collapsed in late 1918, they began planning for an insurrection in Berlin, procuring arms for workers and drawing up plans for an occupation of key political and military sites in the capital.

They picked a date, November 11, for their fourth wave and for the beginning of the revolution in Berlin, which turned out be two days too late. A last-ditch attempt by the German navy to attack the British fleet in the Baltic before armistice led to a series of mutinies in the North, spreading from ship to workplace, from workplace to barracks. Trains carrying arrested sailors were freed by groups of workers, who declared the republic of soldiers' and workers' councils on the spot. In town after town, general strikes were declared independently, with the workers marching on the barracks and electing councils. In Bavaria, on November 7, a general strike marched on the barracks and declared the worker's and soldiers' council of the Bavarian Republic. The King of Bavaria fled, spelling doom for the ancien régime elsewhere. The Majority Social Democrats (SPD), who had been trying to hold back the revolution and negotiate a transition to parliamentary democracy with Allied powers, issued an ultimatum to the government calling for the abdication of the emperor by November 8. But by then it was already clear that the revolution would happen in Berlin on November 9, as it did. Events themselves had calendared the revolution, just as Luxemburg had predicted. The police station and prison were surrounded, and Rosa Luxemburg along with hundreds of others freed. Richard Müller led a march of armed Shop Stewards from the prison in Moabit, where he had been incarcerated, to the Reichstag, which they occupied, and there issued a call for the election of workers' and soldiers' delegates to a meeting of the Berlin workers' councils.

Power does not exist in a place, however, and the capture of the Reichstag did not mean the toppling of the state or its armed power. Negotiations between the Majority Social Democrats, the Entente war powers, and Prince Max of Baden, who served as chancellor of the Reich, began even before the kaiser abdicated on November 9, handing power to an interim SPD government. The counter-revolution occurred coincident with, if not before, the revolution, and thus the emergent workers' and soldiers' councils could not wait for a national conciliar assembly to establish themselves as the reigning power. Events in Russia had shown how the slogan "All power to the soviets!" could become a hollow catchphrase. Rather, the councils in Berlin would have to act as the vanguard of conciliar power elsewhere in Germany, even before any coordination had occurred.

The meeting which Müller called took place the next day in a space suitably large for the delegates of the workers' and soldiers' councils of Berlin, the Circus Busch. Here was the potential Berlin Commune, but fast-moving events and the stalling maneuvers of the SPD ensured that it was indeed a circus. This was a Sunday, meaning that workers could not directly elect delegates in their workplaces. Further, as soon as the revolution seemed unavoidable, the SPD had called for the election of soldiers' delegates in the barracks, knowing that these would be more conservative than the workers' delegates. Credentials were hardly checked, so that of the 1,500 delegates in attendance, most were soldiers and many supported the SPD. The results, as such, were equivocal, a volatile compromise between conciliar and republican power, no doubt originating from the antinomies of the conciliar republic concept itself. The meeting ratified the SPD interim cabinet headed by Friedrich Ebert, now called the Cabinet of People's Commissars, in exchange for equal representation of Independent Social Democrats in the cabinet. But it also affirmed that this cabinet was ultimately subordinate to the workers' and soldiers' councils, to the delegate body there established, and ultimately to the base proletariat itself. To solidify this anchoring power, the assembly elected an Executive Committee of the Workers' and Soldiers' Councils, but unfortunately, against Müller and the Shop Stewards' objections, representation within the Executive Committee was split between the SPD, the USPD (Independent Social Democrats), and a cadre of soldiers' delegates, such that the majority of the committee never recognized the authority of the councils themselves or their own authority, seeing themselves as a caretaker government in advance of national elections to a constitutional assembly representing not just the working classes but all classes, as the SPD had proposed. But the Circus Busch meeting gave nascent councilards reason to hope their position might be strengthened later, by declaring that "political power is in the hands of the workers' and soldiers' councils" and giving chairmanship of the Executive Committee to Shop Steward Richard Müller, who vehemently rejected the election of a national assembly and argued for a conciliar worker's government.[40] It also, much more radically, mandated election of officers and supervision-from-below in the army, a tenet anathema to the generals with whom the SPD was trying to negotiate demobilization.

Resolution of this fundamental contradiction, between bourgeois republic and conciliar republic, or perhaps between the concept of the republic and the concept of the councils themselves, was postponed by the Circus Busch meeting, which took no position for or against a constituent assembly, effectively leaving that decision to a nationwide Congress of the Councils to be held in December. But the SPD had the advantage over the Spartacists, the USPD, and the Shop Stewards, using their power within the cabinet to prevent any radical change of protocol or personnel in the Reichstag and within the Executive Committee to prevent the organization of any effective resistance to the renewed state. In addition to the obstruction of the SPD and conservative soldiers' delegates, the Executive Committee was overburdened from the start with contradictory responsibilities deriving from the status of Berlin as commune, as fragment of a future communism. The fate of the revolution hinged

40 Quoted in Pierre Broué, *The German Revolution, 1917–1923*, Historical Materialism Book Series, vol. 5 (Leiden: Brill, 2005), 152.

on what revolutionaries in Berlin did, and, because of the concentration of military power in the capital, decisive battles were fought there much earlier. The Executive Committee was forced to act for the councils and against the state. As Pierre Broué puts it, the EC "claimed simultaneously to supervise and control the cabinet of the Reich and the Prussian government, to give political leadership to the Berlin council, to act as a centre for the 10,000 councils in the country, to settle labor problems, and to provide a revolutionary orientation on affairs in general," none of which it could do well.[41] Split between a focus on the state and the organization of conciliar power, it quickly became a bottleneck to the latter. Rather than disciplining and restraining the state, it in fact provided ideological cover for Ebert and the SPD's consolidation of power. For example, in declaring that "all orders which come from these authorities will be regarded as being in the name of the Executive Council," they were as much conducting "an attack on the powers of the Council of the People's Commissars" as they were at the same time giving "involuntary support to the attempts to salvage the state apparatus, which was to cover itself with the authority of the Executive of the Councils, in order first to survive and then to retaliate."[42] The Executive Committee was not the expression of a dual power, but a unary power in which its own attempts to wrest control from the Reich further subordinated it to the state. The result was a "two-faced government, soviet for the workers, bourgeois and legal from the standpoint of the state apparatus, the ruling classes, the Army and the Entente."[43]

Outside Berlin, in the interregnum between the November Revolution and the December Congress, the SPD quickly began to consolidate their position within the delegate structure of the councils. Though communists and other intransigents dominated many of the workers' councils throughout most of the industrial heartland of Germany and beyond, where demands for direct workers' power and socialization were made, such as in the industrial heartland of the Ruhr, the algebra of delegation left them represented by weak

41 Ibid., 174.
42 Ibid., 175.
43 Ibid., 168.

allies or by enemies. While the workers' councils in Berlin and in other communist strongholds managed to exclude all delegates not directly elected from the workplaces, such that even Liebknecht and Luxemburg were barred from attending, elsewhere there were no such scruples. Of the nearly 500 delegates, Broué writes that there were "405 sent by workers' councils, and 84 by those of the soldiers."[44] But of those 405 delegates only 179 were workers, the others being journalists and professionals. The meeting that resulted from these canvasses is described broadly in the literature as an act of collective suicide, "a political suicide club" in the words of Müller. Where the Spartacists had hoped that the delaying maneuvers of November 10 might temporarily invest Ebert and the ministers with a power that the councils could eventually retrieve, instead the converse occurred, and the Congress of the Councils effectively ratified the Popular Republic, retaining no powers for itself beyond the power to convene a constituent assembly. There would be no central council from which the organization of the revolutionary economy might unfold.

In retrospect, we might say that Müller, Emil Barth, and the Shop Stewards had failed to heed Luxemburg's central lesson in "The Mass Strike" during their planning of the November insurrection, exerting wasted effort on calendaring a final insurrectionary push whose date the masses themselves determined. They had a plan for the insurrection but not a plan for success. In his biography of Müller, Ralf Hoffrogge notes the vagueness of Müller's call for a soviet, which gave little instruction for how the election of delegates should take place, allowing the SPD to easily game the Circus Busch meeting. In any case, the complicated dialectic between the Stewards Movement and the unfolding mass strike cuts through many preconceptions about the relationship between spontaneity and organization. Planning and voluntary commitments emerge from and feed back into the fires of the mass strike with different kinds of consequences, as the rest of the sequence will confirm.

As events escalated in December, neither Müller and the other representative of the Shop Stewards nor Luxemburg and Liebknecht, among the Spartacists, thought that the time was ripe for insurrection. The defeat of the Congress of Councils had convinced

---

44 Ibid., 184.

them that a hard season of preparatory and organizational work lay ahead of them, but some faction of the revolutionary proletariat, not knowing how much had already been lost, simply would not accept the ascension of the Majority Social Democrats. Struggles around the demobilization of the army and control over the Berlin police department, which stood to pass into the hands of the Social Democrats, as well as the fate of the roving free militias (freikorps), led the EC to call for a general strike whose numbers and intensity surprised nearly everyone. The demonstration on January 5 was perhaps the largest proletarian action that had ever occurred. Two hundred thousand swarmed central Berlin, surrounding the police headquarters, armed, ready to fight, and awaiting the signal. The leaders were not sure how to respond to this surprising show of force, which wanted to be more than show. Broué quotes from the following description of the day, in *Die Rote Fahne*:

> The masses returned sadly homeward. They had wanted some great event, and they had done nothing. And the leaders deliberated. They had deliberated in the Marstall. They continued in the police headquarters, and they were still deliberating. The workers stood outside on the empty Alexanderplatz, their rifles in their hands, and with their light and heavy machine guns. Inside the leaders deliberated.[45]

The self-organizing action of the proletarian masses, suddenly ready for revolution, introduced a scission within the communist leadership, a gap in time and place. Both masses and leadership lay as if under a spell, waiting for the right sign from their counterpart. The show of force convinced some of those debating at the police headquarters that they could now depose the Ebert government, but others doubted that they could hold Berlin for more than a few days. All agreed that simple retreat was impossible—the enthusiasm of the proletariat had to be conserved. The pro-revolutionaries, including Liebknecht and many of the Shop Stewards, who just the day before had agreed with Luxemburg and Müller that conditions were not yet ripe, were allowed to form a committee, which would depose

45 Ibid., 242.

the government if allowed and which typed but did not circulate a communication assuming power.

Liebknecht and others had made their decision after having been told that the Revolutionary Volksmarine (People's Navy), housed in the Marstall, the army headquarters, would support the insurrection. But when their revolutionary committee went to the Marstall they were evicted by the Volksmarine, who had not been fully consulted. The Majority Social Democrats readied their forces for counterattack and violently reconquered the Berlin buildings occupied by the Spartacists and their allies. Thus was the bourgeois Weimar Republic consecrated with the blood of the workers.

In her final assessment of the uprising, "Order Reigns in Berlin," written shortly before she was assassinated by the freikorps along with Liebknecht, Luxemburg lays the blame for the defeat of the Spartacist Uprising at the feet of history—this was or will have been a necessary defeat, a "school" as she wrote twelve years earlier, an expression of the political "immaturity" of the German proletariat the consequences of which would force maturity. Her movementist theory of history is able to treat any failure as a step on the path to success. For Luxemburg, the proletariat was both too revolutionary and not revolutionary enough—it had to resist the provocation which confronted it but was unable to go all the way to revolution. But is hard to know how "leadership" might have succeeded in such a state of affairs where, according to Luxemburg, failure was the precondition for real success, inasmuch as it served as a form of mass revolutionary education.

In that final article, Luxemburg points in particular to the hesitation of the revolutionary sailors, whose support Liebknecht and Georg Ledebour and other members of the revolutionary committee thought they could count on but who balked at the prospect of open civil war and, in fact, ejected the committee from the Marstall. Throughout this sequence, it was the question of the army and the soldiers' councils which disordered the revolutionary parties and the rising proletariat, raising a challenge to which Luxemburg and those in her party had no answer. The German revolution was above all an antiwar revolt, and workers who felt ambivalent about parliament were nevertheless certain they wanted the army abolished. This was, in fact, the only area where the December Congress of the Councils *was* radical—issuing a series of measures that were, according to Broué, "a real sentence of death on the old army: abolition of marks of rank, abolition of discipline and of wearing uniform when off-duty, abolition of external marks of respect, election of officers by the soldiers, and transfer of army command to the soldiers' councils."[46] Ebert and the SPD needed the cooperation of the existing army leaders in order to demobilize but also to hold back any revolutionary excess—needed the remnants of the imperial army to participate, improbably, in their own dissolution, while the broad majority of proletarians, however, opposed any reconstitution of the army or premature disarming of the councils. Demobilization was a complicated and tricky affair for the councils too—revolutionaries didn't want to demobilize too quickly and lose the support of the soldiers' councils and their garrisons. Demobilization might benefit Ebert and the socialist right, who could rely on the freikorps—the mercenary militias, formed from the recently demobilized, who could be deputized by the state and put to work where army and police were absent. The revolution was in the unfortunate position of affirming a social fraction—soldiers—which it would need to abolish.

The KAPD, the Factory Groups, and the Red Army of the Ruhr

The January insurrection was not limited to Berlin and elsewhere continued, even after being crushed in the capital. In Hamburg, Jan Appel, who had organized strikes within the armament industry since 1917 and become chairman of the Shop Stewards Movement there, learned about the killing of Luxemburg and Liebknecht and led a night march to a nearby barracks, whose soldiers they surprised and disarmed, distributing weapons to the 4,000 workers. But the unions managed to demobilize and disarm these workers, and from this experience, Appel and others within the Stewards Movement, as well as many Spartacists, drew the conclusion that the unions were useless for the purpose of revolution. New institutions must be formed—workers' councils firmly rooted in the workplace, free from trade union influence, rigorously proletarian, and

46 Ibid., 231.

unflinchingly revolutionary. To prepare for these, special factory organizations should be constructed on the model of the Stewards. Unlike many of the Shop Stewards and Spartacists, including Müller and Luxemburg, who were willing to risk betrayal in order to keep in contact with the masses, Appel and his comrades within what would eventually be called the KAPD rigorously rejected working with parliamentary parties or trade unions.

In his 1921 speech to the Third Congress of the Comintern, given under the party name Max Hempel and on behalf of the KAPD, called to accounts for its choices during the March Action that year, Appel draws a sharp line between the idea of the council and the Bolshevik theory of revolution.[47] He's had time to witness the course of the revolution across a series of failed insurrections, and from this and a wider survey of the revolutionary wave since 1917 he observes how "the revolutionary proletarian masses form up in struggle." In Russia and Germany, the soviets and councils have become "the organizational form of the masses." The old organizations of the working class—trade unions, parliamentary parties—only sufficed for a period in which the working class struggled to improve its position within capitalism but not to overcome it. When millions of workers call for revolution, however, such mechanisms and the persons attached to them are by their very nature an impediment, and revolutionary workers are naturally drawn to the form of the workers' councils. And "if this is how the proletariat forms up in revolution," Appel tells the Comintern, "then that is how we as Communists … should undertake to organize the revolutionary proletariat."

The work of the communist party is exemplification, the transmission of revolutionary examples "in a manner consistent with the development of the revolution to this point." Communists learn from and lead by example. A council is not just a council but, in a revolutionary conjuncture, also a commune, the future form of communism made present in a fragment of now. It spreads through imitation and exemplification. Winning the masses to the side of

47 John Riddell, ed., *To the Masses: Proceedings of the Third Congress of the Communist International, 1921*, Historical Materialism Book Series, vol. 91 (Leiden: Brill, 2015), 448–57.

revolution was not enough, nor would the formation of a dedicated cadre of professional leaders suffice. Rather workers must be directly given the means by which to exert power. The party, for Appel, is neither a quantitative form, swelling with masses, nor a qualitative one, deepening with discipline, but a catalyst, a vanishing mediator that gives way to direct workers' power. The goal of the KAPD, then, as it distinguished itself from the Bolsheviks in the KPD, was strictly the revitalization of conciliar power and the destruction of all those who stood in its way, specifically the SPD-affiliated trade unions, who by the end of 1919 had locked themselves into the delegate structure of the councils. Militants in the KAPD focused on the formation of *unionen*, or factory groups, structures parallel to the councils but oriented toward them, that might agitate for conciliar power both within and beyond the councils. Rather than seek to organize above the councils, communists should organize alongside them: "Communists must act now to form themselves into a nucleus and a framework that the proletariat can fit into when the conditions draw it into struggle." This notion of leadership, which sees the party as providing a framework, a nucleus, derived from the proletariat's own actions, is markedly different from that of the educating party of Luxemburg or the professional party of the Bolsheviks. Here it is simply a set of founding principles, like the unionen, a model, like the councils, which the proletariat not only can take up but, in fact, must take up "because it cannot any longer struggle through and with the trade unions."

At the time, Appel and his comrades thought a party of organized communists was necessary in addition to the unionen—this is because he recognized the centrality of struggles among the unemployed, who would not find a role within the unionen, but who could be encouraged to organize themselves into councils directly and thereby join with workers' councils.[48] The unionen were open to any revolutionary workers, regardless of affiliation, as long as

48 Many of the most radical adherents to the project of council communism both in the late years of the German Revolution and, later, in the Netherlands and in Germany, were unemployed workers. Paul Mattick, for example, when he brought the legacy of council communism to the United States and attempted to organize according to its insights in the Great Depression, worked largely and primarily with the unemployed. Marinus van der

they agreed on the goal of communism. The party, on the other hand, required that adherents agree with its principles. This division between unionen and party split the difference between mass party and professional party—the unionen were mass communist organizations, whereas the party took up particular positions and postures. This structure meant, however, that the KAPD didn't always have much traction within the factory groups—anarchists had their own unionen, and within the factory groups associated with the KAPD there were many anarchists and communists who did not see the need for a party. Indeed, Appel's later associates within the Dutch-German Group of International Communists (GIK), with whom he would develop, workshop, and publish the *Fundamental Principles of Communist Production and Distribution*, came to find a party redundant or even counterproductive.

Seen another way, however, perhaps redundancy was the point—where the councils failed, there the factory groups could hold firm. Where the factory groups failed, there the party would be unyielding. This was effectively the role which the KAPD played in the revolution, when it played a role at all. As party, its adherents were most effective when operating through loosely coordinated, autonomous armed groups, which tasked themselves with extending and defending moments of insurrection while reproducing themselves through expropriations. This was specifically the case during the 1921 March Action, which represented the height of the KAPD's very limited effectiveness and its last chance at revolution. The March Action was part spontaneous uprising and part coordinated response to this uprising by the armed groups of the KAPD and KPD, like the well-known one led by Max Hölz, or the less-well-known one headed by Appel's associate Karl Plättner. Throughout 1920 and 1921, as the economic situation deteriorated, communists in the KPD and the KAPD were looking for the next insurrectionary moment, not wanting to miss their chance, as they had the year previously, during the 1920 rising in the Ruhr. The flash point this time emerged to the east, in Halle and Mansfeld, where the unionen were quite active and the workers armed, especially in the ultramodern Leuna

---

Lubbe, the council communist who burned down the Reichstag, spent most of his years drifting from job to job and organizing with the unemployed.

works, where according to one estimate at least 2,000 of the 25,000 workers were organized in the AAUD factory group. When the government tried to disarm the workers, a general strike spread through the region, and with rare synchrony both the KAPD and the KPD decided that the time for insurrection had come. This was the high point of heroic ultraleft adventurism. Responding to the general call, the armed units began burning down police stations and courthouses, robbing banks, and distributing expropriated goods. Max Hölz, the so-called Robin Hood of the revolution, ambushed the police units sent from Berlin to put down the rebellious workers in Mansfeld. Here is a description of his proto-communizing force in action:

> A motorized squad had between 60 and 200 men. A reconnaissance unit proceeded in advance, armed with machine guns or small arms; and then came the trucks with heavy weaponry. Then came the commander in his own car "with the strongbox," along with his "secretary of the treasury." As a rearguard, another truck loaded with heavy guns followed behind. All of these vehicles were covered with red flags. Upon arriving in a town, supplies were requisitioned and post offices and banks looted. The general strike was proclaimed and largely paid for by the business owners. Butchers and bakers were compelled to sell their goods for 30% or 60% less than the normal prices. Any resistance was immediately and violently crushed. Such units were very active throughout Saxony after the Kapp Putsch.[49]

The KPD and KAPD central committees issued a general call to insurrection, but beyond that had little control over fast-moving events. Messages got lost in the relay between the center and the provinces. Armed groups operating autonomously had little sense of what was happening elsewhere. In a signal example of the general lack of coordination that prevailed, the semiskilled workers at the occupied Leuna plant resisted the call to take up the arms they had and pass over into the offensive because they concluded they would

49 Gilles Dauvé and Denis Authier, *The Communist Left in Germany: 1918–1921*, trans. M. DeSocio (Baltimore: Collective Action Notes, 2006), 146, available at libcom.org.

be massacred. They were unaware, however, that Hölz's force was nearby and might have come to their aid. Eventually the factory was bombed, the workers disarmed, Hölz captured and arrested. The moment had been lost.

The moment had been lost again, in truth, as the March Action was in some sense an echo of a more general strike and uprising in the region a year earlier, which had led to the founding of the KAPD and defined its understanding of its role. The 1920 uprising, or March Revolution, came in response to the first attempt by the developing right-wing forces around General Lüttwitz to take power through military force. This coup would have been successful if it were not for the spontaneous resistance of the German working class in Berlin, undertaken despite the vacillations of their leaders. Most army leaders neither supported the coup attempt outright nor resisted it through force, and so the SPD and its ministers fled Berlin, seeking a general who might offer them haven. Given the previous betrayals of this government in flight, who had courted and therefore emboldened the very elements which now were ready to displace it, the nascent KPD was ambivalent and did not issue a call to defend the government through a general strike. But the German working class, already organized as a fighting force, was as opposed to the reconstitution of the army and empire as it was to anything and downed its tools without waiting to be told to do so. In Berlin, the new government could print neither money to pay workers nor propaganda to defend its actions, because the printers were on strike. In the Ruhr region and in Saxony, the workers armed or re-armed themselves and issued the call to elect delegates to councils. Max Hölz and his improvised Red Army burned police stations, opened jails, and expropriated currency from banks throughout the rural Vogtland-Erzgebirge region. The coup now seemed to the army and the bourgeoisie to dangerously embolden and concentrate the forces of the left. But events could not simply be rewound on the spool of history—the forces unleashed by the general strike would not accept a simple return to the previous status quo.

This was especially true of proletarians in the Ruhr mining region, where a mass strike of Spartacists and other communists in support of the councils and socialization had been violently disarmed by the freikorps and its SPD handlers in the spring of 1919. Whereas, in

Berlin, a build-up of armed state power made insurrection impossible, power was more dispersed in the Ruhr. Located to the east of the Rhine, the Ruhr was, like Pennsylvania in the United States, an area rich in both iron ore and coal deposits and therefore a natural site for German heavy industry. These were labor-intensive industries and required manpower drawn from every part of the German empire, including Poles from the Slavic regions and Catholics from the south, who had their own unions. Housing in the area was deeply lacking, such that after the revolution, unemployed workers in the steel-producing and metal-working regions of the Ruhr who had been providing for the war effort could not migrate to the nearby coalfields, which wanted for workers, as there was nowhere for them to stay and no transport to get them there. Because of this population density and the general immiseration, the region suffered desperately for lack of food during the war, and many spent the last year subsisting entirely on turnips. After the November Revolution, the most radical councils distinguished themselves by expropriating and redistributing foodstuffs which had been hidden away by employers or rich individuals, whether for their own purposes or to use as incentive. Here the vast wealth of Germany's richest industrialists confronted the misery and squalor of the working class, in the form of massive industrial plants, like the Thyssen complex, which had its own coalfield, its own coke refiners, and blast furnaces for working up coal and iron ore into steel. Thus demands for socialization of production were particularly loud here, and especially so in the western and northern parts of the Ruhr where the anarcho-syndicalist groups were active. But the SPD had preemptively formed councils in other regions, where they cooperated with town administrators, and formed security guards on behalf of the employers. Anarcho-syndicalists, communists, and Independents fought bitter battles for control of the councils in the Ruhr during the strike wave of early 1919, which in several places passed from general strike into civil war, as the SPD commissioner for the region and the Reichswehr, together with the freikorps, disarmed the councils by force, killing dozens. The central demand of these strike waves, in February and April, was socialization of the coal industry, something that the Congress of the Councils had proposed. In Essen, a structure for the socialization of the mines through delegate structures had been approved, and the employers' premises occupied for an initial attempt at implementation, but the Essen model was something of a compromise position developed by Independent Social Democrats to forestall the more radical socialization imagined by syndicalists and communists in the factory groups—socialization according to the Essen model would pass through nationalization and even retain private ownership for a while, while combining this with workers' control.[50] Though councils and delegates were elected, the ambiguity about the role of such delegates led their power to be gradually weakened until they were advisory at best.

The working class in the Ruhr, then, was unusually combative, but it was also the case that the state and particularly the army were very weak locally. As a condition of armistice, the Allies occupied the west bank of the Rhine, along with three key bridgeheads into the rest of Germany; the Treaty of Versailles, signed in 1919, stipulated the demilitarization of the entire Rhineland, including parts of Ruhr Valley. For this reason, the local army commander, Oskar Von Watter, and his SPD counterpart, Carl Severing, were forced to rely on freikorps units to maintain order, units that had been used to brutal effect against the pro-conciliar "socialization" strikes of 1919. Von Watter's initial declaration of neutrality rather than loyalty in response to the Kapp Putsch seemed to many in the region an implicit endorsement, and though he later indicated support for the SPD government, it was already too late. The response by proletarians in the region was swift and powerful: one of the most incredible examples of proletarian self-organization ever—within a few days, nearly 100,000 workers had armed themselves, disarmed freikorps units in Dortmund, and called for the election of delegates to workers' councils. By the time Kapp fled Berlin, this "Red Army of the Ruhr" controlled the entire region from the Ruhr River to the Lippe and had defeated in open battle the Reichswehr units sent from Münster, gaining even more weaponry, including a small air force. The events of a year later, the so-called March Action, were more limited in this respect and did not involve anywhere

50 Jürgen Tampke, *The Ruhr and Revolution: The Revolutionary Movement in the Rhenish-Westphalian Industrial Region, 1912–1919* (London: Croom Helm, 1979), 117–31.

such total mobilization. Here at least were the preconditions for communism—the organized violence of the state shattered by an armed proletarian majority. But this was again a majority divided, unsure of not only its methods but its objectives. Was it merely to defend the Berlin government, the status quo, and the very condition that had brought them there? Or was it now possible to take up aims and arms non-reflexively, seeking not just defeat of the coup but conciliar insurrection? In their willingness to fight to the bitter end, many and perhaps most of the armed groups thought so, but their leadership, constitutively oriented toward compromise and negotiation, did not.

After that first week, a complicated détente emerged—in the rest of the country the putsch had failed, beaten back by the general strike, and armed confrontations had for the most part been limited, allowing workers to retain their arms. In the Ruhr, however, the workers had assumed de facto power and would not give it up, at least without assurances that they would not be massacred. Indeed, many units treated as treasonous all negotiated agreements to disarm, and either ignored them or actively attacked the leaders who had signed. The problem of consensus was in some respect geographical—in the western Ruhr trade unions "were either weak or nonexistent, because the labor force consisted largely of rootless and transient men, many of them Poles and Russians."[51] Where the trade unions were weakest, and where ersatz employers' unions operated, the factory groups of the communists, and also the anarchists, had more success, and had been organizing since the 1919 socialization strikes. In the eastern part of the valley, however, where all negotiations took place and which was closer to the bulk of the Reich army forces arrayed against the Ruhr proletarians, the trade unions and the SPD and the Independents had deeper roots in the workplaces. Most parties to negotiation came from such established groups, partly because the SPD commissioner, Severing, refused to treat with any combat organizations and would meet only with political representatives from trade unions and parties, and partly because the communist left in

51 Werner T. Angress, "Weimar Coalition and Ruhr Insurrection, March–April 1920: A Study of Government Policy," *Journal of Modern History* 29, no. 1 (1957): 3.

the region was too busy arming itself and disarming the enemy, as well as making preparations for the conciliar republic. The unionen were "unitary organizations" not only because they aimed for a single revolutionary council organization both political and economic—organizing not just production but all of life—but also because they refused the division of the workers' movement into trade union and political party, economic and political demands. Such divisions were impracticable in the topsy-turvy of the mass strike but also allowed for substitution and duplication.

There was therefore no single "Red Army" except inasmuch as some political figures designated themselves its representatives. The spontaneous acts of arming and disarming meant that there was no real central military command, much less a political leadership for it—one would have to be formed. In Bielefeld, on March 23, representatives from the councils, town mayors, and delegates from the parties and trade unions met with Severing and Von Watter to negotiate a truce. An action committee in Hagen had already issued demands—that the Reichswehr withdraw and that public order be put in the hands of workers' militias. In Bielefeld, workers' representatives (largely drawn from the Majority Social Democrats, the Independents, and the newly formed KPD) agreed to a plan for phased disarmament but, at the very same time, Red Army units in the west assaulted the fortress at Wesel, where the closest Reichswehr units were stationed. The Red Army in defense of democracy could not itself be democratic—likewise, calls for proletarian democracy could only be calls to revoke the power of the false delegates speaking in their name, something done quite easily by simply breaking the ceasefire without waiting for a show of hands. For the unionen active in the coalfields of the western Ruhr, such as the factory groups leagued with anarcho-syndicalist FAU or the communist AAU (founded only in February 1920), which included future members of the KAPD, there could be no unitary Red Army in advance of elections to councils. But that then meant that for such councilards, defense of proletarian democracy required one-sided and even dictatorial action.

Divided as it was, however, a real proletarian power did exist for a few weeks in the Ruhr, with its hands on some of the chief implements of the German and indeed the entire European economy. We might even call it a conciliar power, if we are clear about what kind of councils were in operation and what kind of power it was. For the most part, no real workplace councils existed in much of the region. This is why communists, Independents, and anarchists called for the re-election of delegates from the workplaces, since in many cases the councils that existed had little relationship to the workplace. It may be worth reviewing how councils were formed during the November Revolution as it spread outward from the sailors' mutiny at Kiel. In the Ruhr, as elsewhere, local power was sometimes deposed by commissions of striking workers who disarmed the authorities, but more frequently the climactic moment occurred when a delegation of revolutionary marines arrived from Kiel, disarmed the police, removed the mayor, and called for the formation of councils. The composition and content of such councils were highly contingent on who was around. Oftentimes, members were elected not from workplaces but from the various parties, with or without proof of proletarian work history. They often worked directly with the town administrators and formed "security guards" more or less loyal to the employers. These were bourgeois councils, fully recuperable by the liberal democratic state and perhaps useful, ultimately, to the process of republican state formation.

Calls to elect delegates from the workplace were thus, implicitly, calls for the workers to retain their arms and their autonomy and for the destitution of the National Assembly. They were a negative demand (recall of delegates) hidden behind a positive one (elections), since any elected delegates who were not in favor of the councils and socialization would be rejected. But this would also mean that, for the time being, army units would have to accept that they were, in fact, such councils. As Dauvé and Authier write:

> The proletarians were victorious as long as they relied upon their social functions, utilizing the productive apparatus for supplies, arms and transport, without, however, remaining within the boundaries of production. The rebel cities united and sent help to the workers in other cities. But even in this respect the movement displayed its weak points, which characterized the whole epoch. After having emerged victorious from its clash with the Army, using the Army's own methods and fighting on its own terrain, the proletarians, in their immense majority,

> thought that their job was done and handed over their power to the parties and the democracy. The red army expelled the military and then transformed itself into the classical workers movement. The workers had mobilized for democracy, and those who wanted to go further were mowed down by the same military force which had supported the anti-democratic putsch and to which the State rapidly turned.[52]

From the perspective of the unitary organizations, it was the very division between political and economic power, army and council, which was the problem, something confirmed by Severing and Von Watter's refusal to negotiate directly with military units. In Duisburg, for example, "the ultra-leftist Wild decided to seize bank accounts and foodstuff, and called for the workers' councils to be elected exclusively from those 'who stand for the dictatorship of the proletariat.'"[53] In other words, they established themselves as a power and mandated a particular *content* and not just a form to the councils. Here was what was missing in the democratic, pluralist conception of the council—delegates who were non-revolutionary or non-proletarian were not delegates at all but rather false substitutes. The delegates must be workers themselves, and they must be explicitly communist. Only where such content is specified can the council as form succeed.

Councils are structures of belonging, community. They link proletarians to the locations where they work and live, and to particular masses of fixed capital to be expropriated, with which individual proletarians have specific history (housing, means of production). Armies on the other hand are universalizing and equalizing bodies, leveling differences, and requiring no history or belonging. Armies organize non-belonging—those displaced by war, catastrophe, or revolution itself—which is why the refugee camp is structured like an army. The defining feature of the army is uniformity—commonalities of dress, speech, and protocol which distinguish friend from enemy and indicate the velocity of command. In the March Action, the armed groups of the KAPD took on this leveling role differently but took it on nevertheless—Max Hölz's expropriators would pay

52 Dauvé and Authier, *The Communist Left in Germany*, ch. 12.

53 Broué, *The German Revolution*, 375.

themselves a standard wage, then send the remaining proceeds to the party, where it would be used to support those in the underground. Paul Mattick's friend Karl Gonschoreck, who led a different group, would enter the bourgeois neighborhood of a town, pull all the furniture from the homes into the street where it could be taken by whoever would, and then light the structure on fire, giving as reason the fact that such homes could neither be expropriated nor shared.[54]

However we regard such an action, this moment illuminates the connection between revolutionary army (which levels and equalizes) and revolutionary council (which links people to particular places). In the Ruhr, as with Gonschoreck and Hölz, these armies were not armies in much the same way the councils were not councils. There was no unity across various commands. This was not just a volunteer army, but one that was self-directed. Even when it is composed of volunteers the nature of the army is conscription, for one can have no choice in military matters and some immediacy of decision must be accepted. Where command collapses there is no army, only armed proletariat, but there is also then possibility for a revolution that is the work of proletarians themselves. The Red Army of the Ruhr established the possibility of an alternate path for the councils—not socialization, which would have entrenched the dependence of the councils on the Weimar Republic (socialization here means nationalization), but communization, a direct expropriation of the means of production in an immediately universal manner, already belonging to the everyone of the armed proletariat.

Councils in Comparison

Councils and council republics were declared variously, sporadically, and without synchrony throughout Central Europe and beyond in the 1917–23 period, emerging sporadically and sometimes whimsically as far afield as Seattle and Limerick, São Paulo and Trondheim. In Hungary, in the spring of 1919, a brief-lived council government was formed, radicalizing the councilards in Bavaria, who, lacking

54 Paul Mattick, *La révolution fut une belle aventure* (Montreuil: L'Echappee, 2016), 64.

sufficient depth in the workplaces, reigned emptily as this or that council republic, before they were outwitted, betrayed, or simply destroyed.[55] Across the Alps, in the industrial cities of Northern Italy, a mass strike movement in the Red Biennium of 1919 and 1920 gave birth to a wave of "factory councils" which took a different shape than did those in Russia, Germany, and Eastern Europe. Similar to the contemporary British Stewards Movement, where the council idea also circulated, these were internal commissions, factory committees, which elected delegates in order to conduct strike activity, but there was no inter-factory "soviet" in this case, leaving the unions and the parties to coordinate. The Italian councils were intensive but not extensive instruments, highly localized and tending to culminate in factory occupations and negotiated confrontations with the state and employers rather than insurrectionary explosion. Unlike the councils in Germany and Russia, Italian councils coordinated after the fact, in large national assemblies dominated by the trade unions. But whereas in Germany and Russia the economic project of the councils was sidelined in favor of their transformation into political instruments under the control of the parties and unions, in Italy the economic project of workers' control tended to eclipse the specifically political objectives, and with them any revolutionary prospect.

In the Italian case, too, there was no partial collapse of state power. Italian militarism and wartime immiseration had led to powerful working-class revolts and general strikes—in Ancona in 1914, and throughout the cities of the north in 1917—but the army was largely demobilized by 1919, and no significant working-class agitation had occurred in the military. Uniquely, the Italian Socialist Party had opposed the war, but a reformist wing of the labor movement, heavily embedded within the trade unions, collaborated with the state to repress working-class action during the war. The internal commissions which would form the basis of the Italian factory committees were in fact originally an invention of the reformist metals trade union, FIOM, which the union could use to mediate and channelize working-class dissatisfaction with wartime production. The trade unions had serious competition, however, from the syndicalist union,

55 Volker Weidermann, *Dreamers: When the Writers Took Power, Germany 1918*, trans. Ruth Martin (London: Pushkin Press, 2018).

the General Confederation of Labor (CGILO) and from the smaller anarcho-syndicalist Italian Syndicalist Union (USI), which managed to wrest the factory committees away from the FIOM, turning them into instruments of the mass strike. Syndicalism as a principle does not distinguish between unions as instruments of class struggle within capitalism and against it, tending to see revolution as the overgrowth of working-class power concentrated in the worksites. The specifically economistic orientation of the Italian councils and their neglect of the political aspect of the councils derive, in part, from this aspect of syndicalist theory, not to mention the mediating interventions of reformists. Syndicalist organization is industrial, organizing workers according to industry and only then by region, a posture amenable to class-wide negotiation but not the organization of insurrection or direct production of communism, which would need to coordinate between worksites on a geographical basis, to be commune as much as council.

Anarcho-syndicalism is a response to the narrow economism and antipolitics of syndicalism broadly, not to mention the reformist tendencies of some syndicalists, visible early on in France with the CGT, who joined the "sacred union" during World War I and agreed to suppress strikes. The Italian Anarchist Union (UAI), for example, recognized the limits of the factory councils early on, but lacked a conception of the council as political-economic amphibian, overcoming the distinction between the political and economic through political decentralization and economic coordination. Instead, they suggested the need for a political supplement, writing in July 1920:

> The [factory] councils resolve only a portion of the problem of the State; they empty it of its social functions, but do not eliminate it; they empty the State apparatus of its control without destroying it … The councils cannot accomplish this function and because of that, the intervention of an organised force is necessary, the specific movement of the class which will carry out such a mission. It is only thus that one can avoid the bourgeoisie, kicked out the door in the garb of the boss, come back through the window disguised as a cop.[56]

56 Tommy Lawson, "Anarchists in a Worker's Uprising," libcom.org, March 2021.

This role would have to be played by the UAI itself, as it would be by the Spanish Iberian Anarchist Federation (FAI) fifteen years later alongside the anarcho-syndicalist National Confederation of Labor (CNT). With this position, the Italian anarchists echo strangely the criticism of their putative antagonist within the conjuncture, Amadeo Bordiga, whose distinct variant of Leninism would develop in opposition to Antonio Gramsci's faction within the Italian Socialist Party (PSI), centered around *L'Ordine Nuovo*, which supported the factory councils and adopted a vision of syndicalist industrial organization as adjunct to a revolutionary overthrow of capitalism. For Bordiga, the factory occupations of October and December 1920 were premature, for workers cannot seize the means of production workshop by workshop:

> The working class will conquer the factories—it would be too slight and uncommunist for each workshop to do it—only after the working class as a whole has taken political power. Without that, the Guardia Regia, the carabinieri, and so on—the mechanism of force and oppression at the disposal of the bourgeoisie, its apparatus of political power—will take care of dispelling all illusions.[57]

Bordiga recognizes the difference between the factory councils and soviets, but imagines a course of development very similar to what occurred in Russia, with soviets as political bodies and the factory councils as economic ones:

> Only up to a certain point can the factory internal commissions be seen as precursors of soviets; more precisely, we consider them precursors of the factory councils, which have technical and disciplinary duties during and after the socialisation of the factory itself. The civic political soviet, then, can be elected wherever it is most opportune, and probably in assemblies not very different from the present electoral polls.[58]

---

57 Amadeo Bordiga, *The Science and Passion of Communism: Selected Writings of Amadeo Bordiga (1912–1965)*, ed. Pietro Basso, trans. Giacomo Donis and Patrick Camiller (Leiden: Brill, 2020), 133.

58 Ibid., 128.

For Bordiga, the soviets must restrict political power to proletarians, not just workers, and for this reason, both the employed and the unemployed must be allowed to elect delegates on a regional basis. Bordiga also recognizes that the soviets must be communist in content and for this reason suggests the delegates should come exclusively from the communist party. Bordiga is operating with a theory of proletarian interest in which the factory commissions represent "sectional" proletarian interest—the interests of workers in a particular workplace in improving their own lives—whereas the soviets represent the interests of the class as a whole; delegates can't represent a particular workshop, in this sense, since they must concern themselves with the reproduction of society as a whole.

In light of the differences between the councils in Germany and the councils in Italy, Bordiga's sense of the factory council movement as representing sectional interest had much to do, in the end, with the syndicalist character of the Italian factory councils, in which representatives from unions did represent workers from a particular industrial sector. His criticism falls flat when applied to the German councils and, in fact, echoes Appel's criticism of the German trade unions—even though the Italian factory councils were led by expressly "revolutionary" unions, they were nonetheless adapted toward negotiation with employers and the state, not revolutionary overthrow. Like Korsch, who also authorizes his perspective through a reading of Lenin's *State and Revolution,* Bordiga criticizes the formalism of some councilards, emphasizing the importance of two contents: a class content and a doctrinal one. The soviets must be thoroughly proletarian, and they must be communist. Importantly for later interpreters of the council idea he emphasizes that class is not determined by employment relations but by property relations—proletarians are all those who are "without reserves" (*sinza reserva*), the class of the dispossessed, which contains the class of laborers. This includes the unemployed but also, implicitly, women and others, whether young or old, who do not work. When the workers occupy their workplaces, when they self-organize, they must not and cannot do it for themselves alone. Their products belong to every proletarian, and their doors must be likewise open to all proletarians. If the councils are to be "essentially a working-class government" and "the political form at last discovered under which to work out the economic emancipation of labor," then their mandate is, from the start, a communist one. Delegates who attempt to reproduce capitalism—who vote for a national assembly, for example—are no delegates at all, for they do not represent a proletarian and communist project. They auto-revoke, as becomes obvious once their nominating councils repudiate their decisions, as happened frequently in the German case, whether formally or tacitly.

Where Bordiga goes wrong, however, is in his sense that the party can function as guarantor of this communist content, by putting forward individuals enlightened by their understanding of communist program. There is a technocratic idealism here, which makes communism a function of right thinking, but, as we have seen in Luxemburg, correct decision-making is not just a function of knowledge but also available information. Without mass participation, delegates are incapable of making correct decisions, simply because they have insufficient knowledge of local conditions. Decision-making must be decentralized to the greatest degree possible while still allowing for unitary action. Bordiga's soviets lack reflexivity, inasmuch as they are supervised by the party from above rather than by the councils from below. But there is a way of reading Bordiga against the grain, which will be discussed more thoroughly later, when we examine his reception in France in the 1960s, in which the party is not so much a formal organization as it is a way of naming all those who are committed to communist revolution. In this sense, then, the party would define the fundamental mandate of the soviets and their principle of inclusion: to delegate or be delegated, you must be both proletarian and communist.

What the councils in Italy during the Red Biennium lacked was the capacity for common action. As Trotsky tells us, the St. Petersburg Soviet ratified and consolidated an already existing unanimity. There was nothing to vote on, only practical matters to decide, preparations to be made. So, too, the Paris Commune, and so, too, Berlin—such unanimity is part of the commune. It is easy to develop such unanimity when the task is a mass strike, harder when it is a general insurrection, and harder still when it is the coordination of communist distribution and production. No council system during the 1917–23 period was able to transform the former unanimities into the latter, instead suiciding in republican constitution before reaching such a point. Only in Spain, during the Spanish Civil War, was communist production and distribution really attempted, but in this case there were no councils independent of the unions, and the forms of power from below were unsystematic, ad hoc, and strongest outside the cities or in areas where radicals were concentrated, such as Barcelona. Communism emerged at the margins, unconsolidated, without any common plan or mechanism of self-reflexivity.

In Germany, the councils invested the bourgeois state with power, against the will of their constituents. In Russia, they assisted the Bolshevik takeover of the state, and the use of such as implement for communist transition. Nowhere did they dissolve the power of the state or bridge the divide between economic and political form. So, too, plans for conciliar socialization in Germany as proposed by the Independent Social Democrats in 1919 and 1920 presupposed the existence of the state as helpmeet, mediating conflicts with the partially expropriated bourgeoisie. By developing as political power first, independent of real control over the means of production, the councils assisted in their capture. On the other hand, isolated factory occupations are not control over the means of production, as Italy shows, since such factories are still dependent on market and state. In the one case, extension without sufficient intensification; in the other, intensification without sufficient extension. In one case, a latent republicanism inherited from the SPD; in the other, an economism deriving from syndicalism.

What was required, it seems, were forms of coordination without political constitution—councils would have to coordinate in order to produce for common use, distribute their products to each other and to residents of various districts, and organize defense of the revolution. In conditions where the councils must spread and deepen, any delegated authority would need to be continuously recalled, continuously re-mandated by the base organizations and reconciled with their changing composition and function. Revolutionary coordination emerges after the fact of unsystematic, one-sided action, in order to extend and intensify such action by rendering it as action in common, universal in its objectives.

The rising in the Ruhr gives some detail to the shape of a communist uprising. Workers liberate a particular area, for example, and distribute the fruits beyond it. They invite anyone and everyone to join them in their work. There is a universalizing, leveling impulse that spills beyond the bounds of any enterprise or area. It is only after this arming of the people and this leveling that the formation of factory councils might meaningfully occur—councils which would not be implements of socialization qua nationalization but direct communization, at once linking each workplace to its corresponding region and the entire extent of communism. In conditions where self-appointed leadership wanted to betray the armed groups, lateral, ambassadorial connections between them were as important as delegates. Eventually such coordination can be formalized, but formalization too early renders organization unresponsive to changing conditions. What is needed is less a specific plan than a plan for a plan, an orientation toward action in common that can turn the chaos of the insurrectionary moment into a self-reproducing communism. The Red Army, an army without a center, could have perhaps become the catalyst of such a process, had the general strike against the Kapp Putsch succeeded in destabilizing or displacing armed power in Berlin and elsewhere.

For some participants, the German Revolution and with it the revolutionary wave of 1917–23 failed because the masses didn't want it. For others, it failed for lack of clarity about its objects. For Paul Mattick, the timidity of the masses found its corollary in the weakness of revolutionary theory without the one becoming cause of the other:

> The spontaneous enthusiasm of the workers was more for ending the war than for changing social relations. Their demands, expressed through the workers' and soldiers' councils, did not transcend the possibilities of bourgeois society. Even the revolutionary minority, and here particularly the *Spartakusbund*, failed to develop a consistent revolutionary program. Its political and economic demands were of a twofold nature: they were constructed to serve as demands to be agreed upon by the bourgeoisie and its social-democratic allies, and as slogans of a revolution which was to do away with bourgeois society and its supporters.[59]

---

59 Paul Mattick, *Anti-Bolshevik Communism* (White Plains, NY: M. E. Sharpe, 1978), 93.

This leaves open the question of what relation there is between such timidity and such weakness. The theory of the revolutionary example as described previously reminds us that practice is always its own theory—thus such weakness reflects such timidity but at the same time consolidates it. In other words, some part of the apathy of these workers might have had to do in part with the weakness of what was to be achieved, nationalization of heavy industry rather than real communism. Theory can no more be clarified independent of the rectification of practice than practice can be rectified independent of theoretical clarification, since practice is itself theory.

This is in part Jan Appel's contention in his 1921 speech to the Comintern. By developing a framework based on the proletariat's own action, one can amplify and redouble its spontaneous enthusiasm for the council. The councils would need to become a living example of socialism not mere political bodies. Appel's speech was given during what was, in fact, his second trip to Russia on behalf of the KAPD. He had traveled there in 1920, directly after the KAPD was formed, to testify to the Comintern about the treachery of the KPD leadership during the Kapp Putsch. With the British and American fleets still participating in the blockade of Russia, the only route open to Appel and his fellow delegates was through the North Sea, around the north coast of Norway and through the icebergs of the Arctic toward the Siberian port of Murmansk, from which the American fleet had just departed. They stowed away on a North Sea herring boat, the *Senator Schröder*, whose crew was largely sympathetic to the cause, then hijacked it, inducing a mutiny and navigating the last leg of the route without charts, as revolutionaries must. They arrived in the Russian port on May 1, 1920, and from there went by train to St. Petersburg and Moscow.

They did not, unfortunately, receive a sympathetic hearing in the capital. Lenin greeted the "comrade-pirates" warmly but dismissively, reading to them from the pages of a manuscript he had written partly in response to the founding of the KAPD, *Left-Wing Communism: An Infantile Disorder*. Appel returned to Germany and to clandestine work in the Ruhr, where he was arrested by the French occupying army and deported to Hamburg to stand trial for his maritime piracy.[60] While in jail in 1924, he tells us, he reflected on his experiences and the fate of the revolution, now definitively finished, and "found the opportunity to study Volumes I and II of Marx's *Capital*."[61] Coming to understand the history of capitalism as one of increasing dispossession, and the concentration and centralization of capital in the hands of the ruling class, he was forced to conclude that the Russian Revolution had not annulled dispossession but in fact had exacerbated it. Appel concludes:

> The most profound and intense contradiction in human society resides in the fact that, in the last analysis, the right of decision over the conditions of production, over what and how much is produced and in what quantity, is taken away from the producers and placed in the hands of highly centralised organs of power … This basic division in human society can only be overcome when the producers finally assume their right of control over the conditions of their labour, over what they produce and how they produce it.

Though the debate was raging about the character of the Soviet Union and the New Economic Policy, which for Appel amounted to state capitalism, it was "a wholly new conception to concentrate one's attention upon the essence of the process of liberation from wage-slavery, that is to say, upon the exercise of power by the factory organizations, the workers' councils, in their assumption of control over the factories and places of work."

He is in prison writing this document, coming to terms with the failure of the revolution, at the same time Adolf Hitler is also serving a prison sentence for his role in the Beer Hall Putsch. Whereas conservative elements within the army before 1923 have contemplated an insurrectionary path to power, Hitler from this moment decides

60 The Ruhr region was not only the economic powerhouse of Germany but a vital economic center for all Western Europe, hence the Entente's insistence on demilitarization of the region and its reoccupation by the French following the Ruhr rising. Revolution that had such an area at its center would necessarily become international. Insurrection in the Ruhr and the Red Army's advance through Poland were in hindsight the only two paths for the world revolution. Hence Appel's focus there and its prominence in the best histories.

61 Jan Appel, "Autobiography of Jan Appel," libcom.org, July 22, 2005.

on a parliamentary rather than strictly insurrectionary path to the consolidation of Nazi power. Appel's conclusions are opposite—a communist movement, unlike a movement to reinstantiate class power, can't use those mechanisms inherited from the bourgeoisie; it must root its power in the economic apparatus from which proletarians draw their strength in combat with the capitalist class. Appel takes the manuscript he has produced with him to the Netherlands, fleeing deteriorating conditions in Germany. There he joins with the Group of International Communists, and together they discuss and revise the text over a four-year period, publishing it as *Fundamental Principles of Communist Production and Distribution* (hereafter *Grundprinzipien*) and effectively disseminating it among the council communist milieu as a preliminary program.[62]

What Appel produces is less a plan for common production than a plan for a plan, a "thoroughly expansive" form, provisional and incomplete by design, which can be completed only when realized as a project of the revolutionary councils themselves. The text is a theoretical clarification and refinement not only of his own experience but of a generational experience of communist struggle. It "will have proved its success," as the preface to the GIK publication says, "only when all revolutionary workers have consciously read through its pages and brought the accumulated experience contained therein into practical application in the struggle for the victory of the proletarian cause, the victory of communism!" The recovery of this accumulated revolutionary experience will have to happen one way or another, the easy way or the hard way, with lessons remembered or learned again. The goal of such texts is to conserve the clarity already achieved by past revolution. While this cannot in and of itself produce communism, it can, perhaps, conserve revolutionary energies by allowing them greater focus. In the next chapter, we will examine the GIK's *Grundprinzipien* and assess what those clarities are, the logical contours of communist revolution revealed by the revolutionary wave of 1917–23. Here we can note,

62 Gruppe Internationaler Kommunisten (Holland), *Grundprinzipien kommunistischer Produktion und Verteilung* (Berlin: Neuer Arbeiter-Verlag, 1930). The English translation was not released until 1990: Group of International Communists, *Fundamental Principles of Communist Production and Distribution* (London: Movement for Workers' Councils, 1990).

briefly, that Appel is largely responsible for introducing the idea, central to council communism and the ultraleft more broadly, that the power-from-below of the workers' councils should be exercised through a form of collective accounting, or inventory. In this view, communism is among other things an open ledger, a network of distributed, open books, visible to all and maintained by all. Here is how Anton Pannekoek, who had to be convinced of this point by Appel, describes the vision of the GIK text:

> As a plain and intelligible numerical image the process of production is laid open to everybody's views. Here mankind views and controls its own life. What the workers and their councils devise and plan in organized collaboration is shown in character and results in the figures of bookkeeping. Only because they are perpetually before the eyes of every worker the direction of social production by the producers themselves is rendered possible.[63]

In some sense, this is the very essence of what the councils reveal about communism, what they add to the discoveries of 1871: politics from below cannot be merely about a raising of hands and a counting (or discounting) of people but must involve real control, materialized through an appropriation of the total wealth of society as a matter both of representation and practice, since the two are inextricably combined. If everything belongs to everyone, some part of that belonging will be by necessity virtual, imaginary, since what is counted in such inventories is not only what is but also what might be.

Comparison always runs aground on history. Before 1945, councils form meaningfully only during a small historical interregnum, 1917–23. After 1945, beginning with the Hungarian Revolution of 1956, councils or something like them appear variously but never in an instance where the armed power of the state had been sufficiently fractured, as in Germany and Russia. Some of these cases will be discussed in the final section of this book. When it comes to the

63 Anton Pannekoek, *Workers' Councils*, ed. Robert F. Barsky (Oakland, CA: AK Press, 2003), 27.

pre-1945 period, however, understanding may well proceed better by examination of a revolution in which armed power was fractured but where there were no real councils to speak of, as in Spain during the Spanish Civil War. An examination of the extent of communism in Spain might reveal, then, the particular capacity and necessity of the workers' council, might provide a contrapositive proof of Appel's argument against Radek and the Comintern. In Spain, where social democracy and Marxism were weak, by comparison, socialism developed differently from in Germany and Central Europe. As in Italy, from the time of Bakunin onward, anarchism and republicanism tended to dominate, with syndicalism becoming powerful in the early twentieth century. Learning their lessons from compromises in Italy and elsewhere, anarchists there managed to solidify a revolutionary and antistatist orientation within the main syndicalist organization, the CNT, forming the FAI as a political adjunct to the CNT unions. But Spanish anarchists rejected workers' councils as a transitional, revolutionary form, in part because, in their correct reading of events in Russia and Germany, workers' councils had become political instruments for the parties. When Francisco Franco and other generals launched their rebellion against the Spanish Republic in 1936, the response was something like the Ruhr rising of 1920 but on a much vaster scale: mass militias, mass seizure of workplaces. But because the unions were more or less committed to the insurrection, in this case councils were not explicitly necessary as instruments of the mass strike: workers' committees remained union committees. The anarchist CNT collectivized workplaces where they were strong, socializing production and setting policies for wages, rates, and work conditions, but the unions were not durable institutions for workers' control from below. Production decisions were largely decided from above, by union officials, and as the civil war progressed even the CNT reintroduced managerial prerogatives and disciplinary measures to maintain productivity. Organized industrially, the only possible socialist horizon was nationalization under union control, which would have to be shared with the socialist union, the General Union of Workers (UGT)—essentially state capitalism. Conciliar structures did exist within the anarchist militias and the rural collectives, where a genuine supervision-from-below and even the suspension of money and wages through the organization of local common plans occurred. Increasingly, however, liberals and statist communists solidified their position within the government, blocking further socialization in the cities and subordinating the militias to their authority.

Late in the civil war, within the Workers' Party of Marxist Unification (POUM) and among the anarchist Friends of Durruti, awareness of these organizational impasses did emerge. But the remedies proposed in most cases were too vague. Writing in 1938, after the CNT-FAI militias and collectives have been dissolved, the Friends of Durruti call for a "Revolutionary Junta," elected directly from the unions, to take over the war effort, placing the military under supervision from below.[64] The unions would then be left to direct socialization of the economy. But the Friends of Durruti do not explain why the unions would socialize production when they had failed to do so given the opportunity in July 1936. Even though the CNT was programmatically committed to revolutionary collectivization, it did not want to take power and impose collectivization unilaterally, for that would require them to follow the path of the state communists and suppress the self-organization of the proletariat—as such it left the tatters of the republic in place, leaving it to others to govern, and hoping the collectives and the militias might eventually subordinate the state to their agenda. In this regard, anarcho-syndicalist pluralism repeated the errors of the Executive Committee of the Councils in Germany, which thought it could subordinate the Cabinet of People's Commissars to its will but instead became subordinated to it. Only Grandizo Munis, member of the POUM who worked closely with the Friends of Durruti, offers a solution to the impasses of the revolution which involves workers' councils. In his "Programme of the Spanish Bolshevik-Communists," written after he and his comrades left the POUM, they reinscribe the pluralism of the anarcho-syndicalists within a Marxian commitment to dictatorship of the proletariat, here as the subordination of war and economy to the soldiers' and workers' councils: in the workers' councils comprising revocable mandated delegates, "the true wish of the masses is allowed the freest possible play … These councils will

64 Friends of Durruti, *Towards a Fresh Revolution* (Barcelona: Cienfuegos Press, 1978 [1938]).

have for their task the defence of the conquests of the revolution, the maintenance of public order, and the control of the economy and distribution. Each party will propose its solutions: the masses will decide."[65]

Munis does not say how the councils will organize production, how they will treat the issues of wages, money, markets, and planning. What he proposes is a "thoroughly expansive form," a form that will give shape, through deliberation, to socialized production, beginning with the occupation of workplaces by the workers themselves, something already achieved in Spain to a very great extent, even at this late date. Nonetheless we cannot assume that all solutions proposed by the parties will succeed in producing communism, nor is Munis clear that communist production and distribution must be the basis for unanimous action by councils. A key problem the CNT confronted in collectivizing the economy was "enterprise egoism"—to an extent greater than anywhere else, Spanish workers and peasants really did seize the means of production, bringing factories and farms under direct control.[66] In the relatively self-sufficient agrarian collectives, in Aragon and in Valencia, money was done away with in some places, and production organized for need. Even after the anarchists in Barcelona had been routed, and political power consolidated by statist communists and liberals, these proto-communist forms persisted, in some cases hanging on despite internal contradictions and outside pressures, and in others even flourishing. But there was no unitary architecture for coordination across regions, aside from the unions. Individual collectives therefore sought advantage for their members irrespective of consequences beyond their workplaces. They lacked any means of producing true inter-enterprise solidarity, except for ad hoc distributions after the fact. Planning at the level of industry by the unions tended to intensify sectional interests, forcing

---

65 "The Programme of the Spanish Bolshevik-Leninists," *Fight* 1, no. 10 (September 1937), 4–5, available at marxists.org. Like many of the figures discussed in subsequent chapters, Grandizo Munis will eventually break with Trotskyism and embrace council communism after 1945, forming the Fomento Obrero Revolucionario in France.

66 Loren Goldner, *Revolution, Defeat and Theoretical Underdevelopment: Russia, Turkey, Spain, Bolivia*, Historical Materialism Book Series, vol. 122 (Chicago: Haymarket Books, 2017), 134.

the CNT planners to subordinate the unions to a central planning apparatus which increasingly resembled the state capitalism of the Moscow-aligned communists. The supervision from below of the collectives therefore increasingly faced a pressure from above, forcing them to conform to a heteronomous plan, without any mechanism of reflexivity between the collectives and the planners. As Munis describes it this was less dual power than "an incomplete atomization of political power in the hands of the workers and peasants … limited solely by its lack of centralization and by the right-wing interference of the working-class bureaucracies."[67] Inasmuch as collectives were not intensive instruments of mass participation and inasmuch as they were organized sectorally or by enterprise they could not coordinate meaningfully—intensivity and extension are, Munis reminds us, mutually constitutive.

In Spain, the anarchists lacked focus and a clear vision of success, which contributed to the demoralization of the revolutionary party—but this was true of Germany, too, true of the Spartacists and the Shop Stewards, and true, likewise, of the Italian factory council movement. Spain, we can say, makes clear the consequences of the absence which Appel and others diagnose in Germany—what would have been necessary there were forms of collective accounting and accountability from below, distributed throughout the relevant neighborhoods and workplaces. Nowhere were workers' councils able to overcome the opposition between economic and political form, to become both extensive and intensive organizations—in Italy and Spain, socialization of production by intensive base committees of workers occurred, and in Spain to a very great degree. But they were not extensive organizations of political power, able to dismantle and displace the state as the locus of power and coordinate armed resistance and the reproduction of communism. In Italy, there was no plan for such an extensive organization and political conquest of power; in Spain, where power fell into the lap of the CNT committees, its extensive form was handed over to the unions and parties, with no clear plan for its consolidation in the collectives. In Germany, on the contrary, the extensive councils formalized themselves politically without consolidating real intensive economic power, becoming

67 Quoted in ibid., 128.

essentially an appendage of the bourgeois state. In Spain in 1936, there was no wider revolutionary wave to provide them support, to undermine the enemies of the revolution abroad. On the contrary, Hitler's planes and Mussolini's tanks made Soviet arms and the collaborationist policies that came with them hard for many to refuse. But if we imagine a different international situation, and perhaps a few more military successes for the revolutionary militias early on, what might revolutionaries have done? The proletariat was armed and a large portion of production under its direct control. A project of immediate socialization-from-below, unafraid of police or army repression, perhaps could have stabilized communism. This would require not just revolutionary will, not just clarity about what communism is, but also a distribution of the basic information which the revolutionary proletariat would need to socialize production. In an excellent essay on the Spanish Civil War, Loren Goldner links the lack of revolutionary vision among Spanish anarchists to contemporary Marxist anti-utopianism, which refuses the positing of solutions not immanent to struggles themselves. Echoing Appel, Goldner concludes that revolution then and now would require "an immanent 'inventory' of world material production and above all the material reproduction of those who are engaged in it."[68] Such an inventory, for Goldner, takes stock both of proletarian struggles and the material wealth of society with the goal of understanding how the two can combine to produce communism—in other words, an inventory of this sort would need to be "immanent" to the revolution itself, part of the process in which "all will be judged, and transformed, based on global needs, once true production for use-value, centered on the reproduction of the ultimate use-value, labor power, is possible."

68 Ibid., 149.

2

The Test of Communism

As "thoroughly expansive" forms whose potential remained unactualized, the Commune of 1871 and the workers' councils of 1917–23 hail from the future. When Rosa Luxemburg, Jan Appel, or Grandizo Munis call for the establishment of workers' councils from the midst of a revolutionary sequence they still rate capable of succeeding, they look to an immediate or slightly more distant past and see in it a form able to open the doors to the future. This has the effect of making the theory of the commune both retrospective and prospective at once. For what the partisans of council or commune see in the past is not an actuality but a potential—not a program to be realized but a series of logical requirements and concomitants to be navigated.

The commune and the council show us what is eternal about revolutionary struggle against capitalism—what will always remain true insofar as capitalism and its problems persist. It remains as true today as it was in 1871 that "the working class cannot simply lay hold of the ready-made state machinery, and wield it for its own purposes." Likewise, it remains true that "Paris could resist only because, in consequence of the siege, it had got rid of the army, and replaced it by a National Guard, the bulk of which consisted of working men." What Marx describes as the "first decree" of the Commune—"the suppression of the standing army and its replacement by the armed people"—is actually a precondition of any revolution, realized by the precipitating events of 1871 and ratified after the fact. Only where war, chaos, or crisis has rendered the army intractable to state power do we see the real possibility of communist revolution. This doesn't mean that all aspects of revolution can be deduced logically, but an understanding of what is contingent in revolution requires an understanding of what is not. In this chapter, I treat the theory of communist revolution from the vantage of eternity. In the subsequent chapter, I examine it from the vantage of history, testing this logical theory against class struggle in the present.

At stake here is as much a method for reading history as for reading Marx. Key parts of the history of past revolutions as well as the pages of Marx's *Capital*—and much other revolutionary theory—are illegible except by the light of a communism seen as inevitable, both historically and logically certain. This has the effect of making Marx appear most grandiose where he is in fact most modest. In 1868, he writes of the just-published *Capital*, his critique of political economy, that it is "without question the most terrible missile that has yet been hurled at the heads of the bourgeoisie."[1] "Heads," here, confines his work to the field of discourse. Marx could devote himself to critique, in other words, to sinking the supply ships of bourgeois economics, precisely because he did not think such work determinative in matters of class war. He would hurl books at the heads of the bourgeoisie while the proletarian movement took out their legs.

Take, for example, his letter to his long-time friend and supporter Louis Kugelmann, who wrote to Marx immediately after the original publication of *Capital* in German to report that readers familiar with economic theory were struggling with Marx's theory of value. Marx responds:

> The vulgar economist has not the faintest idea that the actual everyday exchange relations need not be identical with the magnitudes of value. The point of bourgeois society consists precisely in this, that *a priori* there is no conscious social regulation of production. The reasonable and the necessary in nature asserts itself only as a blindly working average.[2]

---

1 Karl Marx, "Letter to Johann Philipp Becker," in Karl Marx and Friedrich Engels, *Collected Works*, vol. 42 (London: Lawrence & Wishart, 1994), 358–59.

2 "Marx to Kugelmann in Hanover," July 11, 1868, in Karl Marx and

The bourgeoisie and its intellectual representatives are therefore forced to treat as "great discovery" the fact that "in appearance things look different." They have no need for Marx's "science" and in fact their standpoint in society will make it difficult to comprehend very simple matters: "The nonsense about the necessity of proving the concept of value arises from complete ignorance both of the subject dealt with and the method of science. Every child knows that a country which ceased to work, I will not say for a year, but for a few weeks, would die." The problem in other words is not so much that Marx is very smart but that bourgeois economists are particularly stupid—their reaction "shows what these priests of the bourgeoisie have come to, when workers and even manufacturers and merchants understand my book and find their way about in it." Notice the emphasis: *even* manufacturers and merchants can understand it, but workers do so more naturally. If his critique of political economy is a missile lobbed at the heads of the bourgeoisie, it is not undertaken to explain capitalism *to them* through the percussion of intellectual missiles—it is a critique on behalf of the working class, who pushes the attack on other fronts.

It is not because workers are better educated about the principles of economics that they intuitively understand Marx's work. Rather it is because the experience of exploitation and oppression daily reminds them of the coherence and correctness of Marx's critique, the necessity of revolution. What he says of "every child" is likely not true of bourgeois children, for whom the products of labor appear as if by magic; but proletarian children, who begin work young and watch their families work, do understand such basic matters. At stake is more than experience, however, but also attitude, standpoint—Marx's *Capital* is always illuminated by a future communism. Once the "inner connection" between value magnitudes and exchange relations "is grasped," he tells Kugelmann, "all belief in the permanent necessity of existing conditions breaks down before their practical collapse." This first collapse, the critical collapse, is neither cause nor precondition of the practical collapse in crisis or revolution. Marx does not believe that by proving capitalism impermanent he will induce the bourgeoisie to simply quit the field. Indeed, he has noted

Friedrich Engels, *Collected Works*, vol. 43 (London: Lawrence & Wishart, 1994), 68.

they will find it constitutively difficult to descry their doom in the fog of the business cycle. Marx in 1865 is tribune of a workers' movement that has already announced its historical mission: to abolish capitalism. It is not that Marx can kill capitalism with his ideas, but that he has expressed in ideas a movement already underway, one which seemed certain to usher in a practical collapse. The point of the critique of political economy is not so much ideology critique as it is an illumination of existing conditions in light of their practical collapse, on behalf of and for the movement that will precipitate it.

Marx wrote a book entitled *Capital*, not one entitled *Communism* or *The Proletariat*, because the workers' movement did not need its ends articulated, did not need an explicit description of classless society, that common horizon. It needed better weapons, a clarification of means. At stake here is less a claim about Marx's method than one about the methods which communists should use to read Marx. We can no doubt treat *Capital* as a grand analysis without presuppositions, an immanent critique, a science, a research project, but certain key aspects will remain inscrutable, written in invisible ink that only the heat of communism can bring to the surface. I think this is the case for important parts of Marx's theory of value. As Marx notes in the letter, the bourgeoisie need hardly bother with the concept of value. They can make do with appearances. If proletarians understand the concept of value more readily it is because value names for Marx the inner coherence of that monster which proletarians recognize as their enemy. Value names the *differentia specifica* of the capitalist mode of production, the one element that presupposes all the others, the ring that binds together the other rings of money and wages, profit and price, property and the police, the state and the banking system, world markets and international conflict. The concept of value is as much a descriptive concept as a revolutionary hieroglyphic, a critical heuristic designed to focus those who would overthrow capitalism on the essential.

These objectives are clearer in Marx's first attempts at critique of political economy, where Marx generally had very particular political interlocutors in mind. Early anti-capitalists such as Pierre-Joseph Proudhon and his disciple Alfred Darimon, on the one hand, and the "Ricardian Socialists" like John Francis Bray, John Gray, and

Thomas Hodgskin, on the other, frequently proposed to right the wrongs of capitalism through reform of the money system and banking.[3] Marx recognized the incoherence and impracticability of these reforms—which mostly consisted of proposals to replace national and bank money with "labor money"—and it was in developing concepts adequate to these critiques, first in the *Grundrisse* and then in *A Contribution to the Critique of Political Economy*, that Marx struck on key aspects of his theory of value.[4]

Labor money was in many respects a derivation from the labor theory of value developed by Adam Smith and then David Ricardo. In the 1820s and 1830s in Britain, as resistance to early capitalism took shape in the form of trade unions and cooperatives, social reformers associated with Robert Owen and then Chartism developed the labor theory of value (LTV) into a theory of exploitation depending on natural rights and natural prices, cast in absolutist moral terms.[5] Once it had been demonstrated that labor is the source and measure of all wealth, it required only a simple step further to propose to right the injustices of capitalism by denominating goods in terms of their "real" or natural value. With the prices of goods labeled in terms of labor hours and labor minutes, rather than dollars and pennies, it would be nearly impossible to swindle workers and not give them the full value of their product, according to proponents of the theory. The LTV thus offered both a critique of capitalism and a way to improve it, subordinating money and capital to the benefit of laborers and, in turn, the nation. Every monetary exchange could be made equal and transparent, with its real value for a producer written right there on its face.

---

3 Alfred Darimon and Emile de Girardin, *De la réforme des banques* (Paris: Guillaumin et Cie, 1856); John Gray, *Lectures on the Nature and Use of Money: Delivered before the Members of the "Edinburgh Philosophical Institution" during the Months of February and March, 1848* (Edinburgh: A. & C. Black, 1848).

4 Karl Marx, *Grundrisse: Foundations of the Critique of Political Economy* (New York: Penguin, 1993); Karl Marx, "General Rules and Administrative Regulations of the International Working Men's Association," in Karl Marx and Friedrich Engels, *Collected Works*, vol. 23 (London: Lawrence & Wishart, 1988), 257–518.

5 E. K. Hunt, "The Relation of the Ricardian Socialists to Ricardo and Marx," *Science and Society* 44, no. 2 (1980): 177–98.

Marx eventually refuted this by demonstrating that such a notion of fair exchange was self-contradictory: the very idea of equal exchange presupposes inequality, as he shows, because the value of *labor* (the output of a worker) is never the same as the value of *labor power* (the reproduction requirement of that worker, and therefore the price of its use by a capitalist). From this distinction, Marx develops one even more fundamental, between concrete labor and abstract labor, the core of his mature theory of value. His main achievement in this arena was not, as is sometimes supposed, a theory of surplus value or a proof of exploitation—versions of such a theory were already available, as he would summarize in the manuscript entitled *Theories of Surplus Value*. As Diane Elson formulates it elegantly in her seminal essay "Value: The Representation of Labor in Capitalism," summarizing debates on the topic in the Conference of Socialist Economists in the 1970s, Marx's theory of value had been radically misunderstood by those who saw in it a method to calculate the magnitudes of exploitation: "It is not a matter of seeking an explanation of why prices are what they are and finding it in labor. But rather of seeking an understanding of why labor takes the forms it does, and what the political consequences are."[6]

Elson worries overtly in her introduction that her corrective reading, distinguishing between Marx's theory of value and the Ricardian LTV, might be depoliticizing. For the Ricardian proof of exploitation, with or without labor money, at least had the virtue of being politically salient and leading to very clear practical objectives. This is because, despite the power of her corrective reading, she does not see how the concept of value is directly connected to the objectives of communism, naming not only a historical process—"why labor takes the form it does"—but a great misfortune, understanding of which will aid in its overcoming. Elson stands at the headwaters of a new way of reading Marx, begun in the 1960s and 1970s, with the publication of Marx's complete works, and sometimes called "value-form theory" or, with respect to German exponents, the "new reading of Marx" (*Neue Marx-Lektüre*). These Marxological interventions have been enormously clarifying for readers of Marx,

6 Diane Elson, ed., *Value: The Representation of Labour in Capitalism* (London: CSE Books, 1979), 123.

making sense of the inner analytic coherence of Marx's work. This clearheaded way of reading Marx has, however, come at the expense of a certain political power, I would argue. It is a way of reading Marx for an era that lacks Marx's certainty.

In the text that follows we will encounter another, complementary way of reading *Capital*, in which Marx's masterwork is not only the adequate representation of the capitalist mode of production but an outline in negative of its overcoming by communism. I have come to this way of reading Marx by a long and winding route, over terrain that will be mapped thoroughly, though its origins lie in the programmatic method of Amadeo Bordiga, for whom, to use Gilles Dauvé's helpful paraphrase, "the whole of Marx's work was a description of communism."[7] Bordiga is supremely attentive to those moments in Marx's mature writing, surprisingly abundant if you know what to look for, where in order to illuminate some feature of capitalism, Marx finds that he must, in fact, compare it with a fictitious communism. "Let us finally imagine, for a change, an association of free men, working with the means of production held in common and expending their many different forms of labor power as one single social labor force."[8] This is offered as ultimate contrast with capitalism, where the fetishism of commodities induces a complicated situation in which humans become mannequins puppeted and ventriloquized by sarcastic commodities, both unfree and deluded about the sources of their unfreedom. The purpose of such contrast is to bring out key features of the capitalist mode of production and class society more generally, otherwise untheorizable. It is only in the light of communism that we come to see the misprisions of the commodity form for what they are: "The veil is not removed from the countenance of the social life-process, i.e., the process of material production, until it becomes production by freely associated men, and stands under their conscious and planned control." Marx therefore offers more than a description of capitalism, but one in which key predicates of communism become visible.

7 Jean Barrot (Gilles Dauvé) and François Martin, *Eclipse and Re-emergence of the Communist Movement*, 1st ed. (Detroit: Black & Red, 1974), 125.

8 Karl Marx, *Capital*, vol. 1, *A Critique of Political Economy* (New York: Penguin, 1992), 171.

At stake here is less a claim about Marx's method than the method that communists should apply to the reading of Marx. For communists, the science of capitalism is the theory of the rules of a game they hope to consign to the dustbin. The goal for us is neither just to enumerate those rules nor to learn to play the game better, but to develop from them an understanding of how the game itself might be overcome. If it is anything for communists in the twenty-first century, it is an applied science, the science of destroying capitalism, whose descriptions of capitalism and predictions about class struggle and its unfolding have their meaning in action, in class struggle itself. And here our concern should be less about what Marx intended—science of capitalism? weapon against it?—than what we, as communists, need. We need to *know* what capitalism is, but not in order to wonder at it and enumerate its sublimities. The concept of value is nothing, for communists, if not a crosshair that flashes red when we need to smash something.

There is also in Marx a *tendential* theory alongside the heuristic theory. The light of communism revealed for Marx a directionality to capitalist production, one that pointed toward its ruin but also its overcoming by communism. The tendencies identified are numerous and complexly entangled: mass proletarianization, immiseration, and increase in superfluous populations, concentration and centralization of capital, globalization of trade, rising organic composition of capital, falling rate of profit, depletion of the soil, colonization, and imperialism. Chief among all these tendencies, however, was the tendency for capitalism to produce its own gravediggers in the rising, militant proletariat. The tendencies are also, it should now seem needless to say, illuminated by a future communism. This is because, first, the rising proletariat is already practically oriented toward communism and, second, tendencies within capitalism lead inexorably toward communism. Tendencies are directional, and directions are not neutral but stained with the dye of class struggle, progressive and reactive.

Some of Marx's tendential theory has not held up, at least if read strictly, and in a few instances, it must be admitted, Marx was badly wrong. But the fact that any of it has held up, even though the communist revolution has not occurred and capitalism soldiers on long after Marx could have thought such a thing imaginable, counts as no small feat. None of his contemporaries fare better. The tendential theory must, in any case, always return to the facts of the world, of class struggle, for confirmation. But it also must know what it's looking for, where it hopes history will lead. Here again Marx can appear most grandiose when he is in fact being most modest. He need not proselytize and inveigh, draw up battle plans and programs, for the tendencies of capitalism are already doing the work of forming a resistance adequate to it. The tendential analysis is not prescriptive but diagnostic, highlighting limits and opportunities. But these are opportunities that, for Marx, the working class must come to understand one way or another. It is class struggle itself which brings these opportunities to mind for Marx—his work is to clarify and refine political tendencies, the communist movement principally, already in the process of formation.

Seen in this new historical light, Marx concludes not only that the proponents of labor money were wrong but also that their proposals would by necessity be rejected, and were indeed already being rejected, by the new proletarian movements sweeping across Europe and the world. Labor money assumes, in its theory of exploitation, an underclass consisting not so much of wage laborers as artisans who own (or borrow) their means of production and sell their output on the market. Such petty producers were exploited by merchants and bankers offering them increasingly miserable terms, threatening them with bankruptcy and, in turn, loss of the means of production, ultimately reducing them to mere proletarians. A reform of the market, offering "fair terms" or a restoration of precapitalist conventions of natural right, appeals to artisans because the market is the locus of their exploitation. Proletarians, on the other hand, are more likely to see their oppression as originating from production itself. As such, Marx wasn't rejecting labor money only on the plane of ideas, as practically unworkable, but also as resting on a pragmatic class basis which made its moral theories of natural right and price inapposite. The labor monetarists thought the way they did, then, according to the theory Marx develops, because of a social division of labor and a historical process (the formation of a strictly propertyless proletariat) which duped them into thinking their own ideas causes when in fact they were simply effects.

In *The German Ideology*, Marx and Engels caricatured their post-romantic contemporaries, "the type of the new revolutionary philosophers in Germany," as being like the proverbial fellow who thought that "men were drowned in water only because they were possessed of the *idea of gravity*."[9] John Gray and Alfred Darimon were thus cut from the same mold as the reactionary, bourgeois, and utopian socialists Marx and Engels took to task in *The Communist Manifesto*, and the various post-Hegelians they savaged in their other writings. Against this, uniquely in the history of radical thought up until then, Marx and Engels developed an account of history which placed class struggle and proletarian self-activity at the center of any meaningful project to overcome capitalism. It was no longer simply a matter of ideas, though ideas were very much at stake, since the matter had to be hashed out in the pages of books. What mattered was class struggle, collective action, social practice.

Once the moral underpinnings of labor money are made apparent, the political implications of Marx's turn to economics and the critique of political economy in the 1850s make perfect sense, coming as it does after the thoroughgoing critique of the moral, religious, and idealist presuppositions of his fellow socialists and communists that he had developed in the 1840s. Diane Elson need not be so worried, then, about losing political salience by casting off the Ricardian fetters of Marxist pseudo-orthodoxy. It's not so much that value analysis renews critical thought or denaturalizes the economy, though it does all this. Rather Marx's value theory offers a method by which certain socialist proposals can be put to the test. This is prediction, but only of a certain sort. It does not tell you what will happen but what must or what can't. The test of value is a logical test—it works from the definition of capitalism, its basic logical structure, in order to clarify what it would mean to overcome it. Here, however, it must be said from the start that the dialectic has betrayed many a traveler to this region, leading some to believe that the abolition of value, the sine qua non of capitalism, is itself the sufficient condition for communism when it is in fact merely a necessary one. Communism *cannot* be derived logically from the presuppositions of capitalism. There is a missing moment, an absent positive, to the inversion of

9 Karl Marx and Friedrich Engels, *Collected Works*, vol. 5 (London: Lawrence & Wishart, 2010), 24.

value. Indeed, that missing moment is what is fundamentally missing from life not just in capitalism but in all class society.

The Test of Value 1: Marx against Labor Money

The crux of Marx's critique is this: the labor monetarists identify as flaws what are in fact integral features of capitalism. There is an ineliminable difference between the magnitude of individual labor exerted in producing a commodity and the magnitude of social labor—that is to say, socially necessary average labor—which the commodity commands on the market. One cannot weld closed this gap except by reforming the economy top to bottom. As long as reformers do nothing more than issue new money with new symbols on its face, market forces will invariably introduce a gap between the stated and real value of a good denominated in labor time. If markets are competitive, and sellers are allowed to change their terms, and buyers to seek out the best price, a ten-hour note earned by a worker will not always command ten hours of labor but more or fewer hours depending on supply and demand. The only way to avoid this problem and still allow market determination of prices (as many of these reformers wished) would be to ensure that supply and demand were always balanced. To do so, however, is easier said than done, as this requires that raw materials, component parts, and labor are always adequately distributed across the entirety of the economy; undersupply of a component or raw material, such as cotton, will necessarily lead to an undersupply of all the goods that incorporate it, such as cotton shirts. The distortions that the reformers hope to eliminate are symptom of a malady located in production itself, cure of which would require restructuring of the entire economy, not just new types of money. Just as today new monetary theories suggest the injustices of capitalism might be overcome through a prodigious unloosening of state credit money, these nineteenth-century reformers mistake cause and effect, hoping to achieve through superficial methods something achievable only through a total overhaul of capitalism. Marx submits their proposals to a test of logic and discovers that they assume their conclusion:

> If the preconditions under which the price of commodities = their exchange value are fulfilled and given; balance of demand and supply; balance of production and consumption; and what this amounts to in the last analysis, proportionate production (the so-called relations of distribution are themselves relations of production) then the money question becomes entirely secondary, in particular the question whether the tickets should be blue or green, paper or tin, or whatever form social accounting should take.[10]

In attacking these schemes, first in the manuscripts known as the *Grundrisse* and then in *A Contribution to the Critique of Political Economy*, he shows that far from proposing to reform capitalism they in fact implicitly describe a world in which it has already been overcome:

> The fact that labour money is a pseudo-economic term, which denotes the pious wish to get rid of money, and together with money to get rid of exchange-value, and with exchange-value to get rid of commodities, and with commodities to get rid of the bourgeois mode of production—this fact, which remains concealed in Gray's work and of which Gray himself was not aware, has been bluntly expressed by several British socialists, some of whom wrote earlier than Gray and others later.[11]

Labor money implies this "pious wish" because it *presupposes* a whole host of other radically transformative measures. Marx demonstrates this by submitting the proposals, as we've seen, to a speculative reductio ad absurdum, what we have called the test of value, and taking the reformers at their word, carefully thinking through the dynamic effect of labor money given his understanding of the *laws of motion* of capitalism. This is a speculative test, in advance of the real test, where "bankruptcy would in such a case fulfil the function of practical criticism."[12]

In these passages, Marx in fact offers two distinct but intrinsically linked dynamics that would scuttle labor money, and the second will

10 Marx, *Grundrisse*, 153.

11 Karl Marx and Friedrich Engels, *Collected Works*, vol. 29 (London: Lawrence & Wishart, 1988), 323.

12 Ibid.

be of more consequence as our story of the communist test of value progresses. Even where supply and demand are in equilibrium, there is another reason the units on the face of a labor note would not necessarily equal the real labor time involved in the production of any given purchase. In the case where producers operate with differing levels of productivity—where, for example, one cobbler requires three hours to make a pair of shoes that another can make in two—then the freedom of producers to set their prices and the freedom of consumers to search out the lowest prices must be absolutely restricted if the face-value of a labor note is to be trusted. Assuming that supply and demand are equal and that producers and consumers are free to do as they wish, the cobbler who can make a pair of shoes in two hours will instead demand as high a price in labor notes as is possible while still managing to undersell competitors, attracting all consumers. The cobbler who requires three hours will, in turn, be forced to lower prices in order to sell anything at all. Thus, the price of shoes in labor notes will equalize around the average labor time required to make a pair of shoes, with the one producer exchanging their shoes for more hours in labor notes than they require for their needs and the other for less.

There are only two ways around such a scenario: either one ensures that every producer is equally productive—homogenizing tools, techniques, intensity of work, and workshop size for every good—or one establishes a situation in which producers cannot price their goods variably and consumers have no choice about which goods they buy. The first scenario would require a momentous transformation of the economy, reconstructing each workshop and totally transforming the scale of production. It would also require, more problematically and more importantly for our critique, the development and enforcement of production norms that could confirm and ensure an equal intensity of work for each person. The second scenario would likewise require a massive surveillance operation, if goods are to be accurately priced in labor hours and minutes. Unlike the first, however, it would generate destabilizing inequality, as producers could receive vastly different incomes for reasons not only to do with how much effort they applied but the tools and equipment which they could access. One worker might earn twice as much as another for the simple reason that they happened to affiliate with a factory twice as productive. Consumers, too, would find their ability to consume dependent upon their place in the queue or other sorting mechanisms, since there would need to be some way to assign different prices to different consumers.

We can summarize Marx's reductio to communism as follows: far from being a simple mechanism of monetary reform that would ensure a fair wage for every worker, labor money in all its guises presupposes a thoroughgoing transformation of the economy. While many proponents of labor money understood that a central bank would need to act as buyer and seller for all goods, Marx showed that the operations needed go quite beyond this. Marx locates in Gray a pious wish for communism, because such a "bank" would need to balance production across all branches of the economy and determine the demand for each type of final and intermediate good, surveil and potentially discipline workers in each workplace, and finally ensure a uniform level of technology across workshops producing identical goods. It would be more than a bank, more even than a clearing house, but rather a planning apparatus able to engage in ex ante control of production, determining all the decisions producers make. Once such a complete reconstruction has been undertaken, Marx implies, the question of labor money will seem quite secondary and perhaps no question at all. Far more important, for Marx, is the question of the oppressive or emancipatory character of the central bank in such a scenario, given the demands upon it. There are only two choices here: Marx writes that "either it would be a despotic ruler of production and trustee of distribution, or it would indeed be nothing more than a board which keeps the books and accounts for a society producing in common."[13] In other words, *either* it would be a planning apparatus desperately trying to overcome through despotism inequalities baked into the material infrastructure *or* it would be a natural apparatus resulting from a society having overcome these inequalities.

The test of value is therefore a logical test, an immanent critique which, given any communist proposal for economy, reveals its presuppositions and from there constructs a speculative developmental course. If the reformers want the money to function as money, then

13 Marx, *Grundrisse*, 155–6.

this means it will need to fulfill certain functions, which presuppose features x, y, and z. If alternatively the reformers want the money to perform a new function—that of equalizing wages around a single measure of wealth—then, as Marx demonstrates, new functions will need to be determined which, by logic, presuppose a material reorganization of the economy. From the science of value, we can develop a critical science fiction of value, tracing out the course a revolution must take by delineating certain logical points of failure, certain guardrails.

The Test of Value 2: Marx against Lassalle

These early writings on labor money are not often discussed, perhaps because they appear to contradict better-known remarks Marx made a decade and a half later, in his "Critique of the Gotha Program," wherein he seems to have accepted that a transitional communist society would use "certificates" to meter and regulate the consumption of individual workers.[14] In this late text, written for internal circulation among his associates, Marx is not by any means offering a positive program, but rather a series of corrections. The later Marx text is also a test of value—in this case, a review of the draft program of the Gotha Unity Congress of 1875, which founded the Social Democratic Workers' Party (SPD) and the mainstream of Marxism by merging the party of Ferdinand Lassalle, Marx and Engels' main socialist opponent in Germany, with the group that Marx's close associates, Wilhelm Liebknecht and August Bebel, had formed. Engels made the text available in 1891, after Marx had died, during a period of party debate about the subsequent program, the Erfurt Program, from which Engels felt he had, with Marx's text and his own polemics, eliminated "the last remaining traces of Lassalleanism."[15]

As before, in this text, Marx is eager to debunk the "Lassallean catchword of 'the undiminished proceeds of labor,'" a nonsense notion as there is no way to arrive arithmetically at a sum that is

14 Karl Marx and Friedrich Engels, *Collected Works*, vol. 24 (London: Lawrence & Wishart, 1989), 75–99.

15 Ibid., 239.

not diminished for some party.[16] There is no such thing as "a fair distribution of the proceeds of labor" or an undiminished one.[17] If all members of society are entitled to equal wealth, then the proceeds cannot be undiminished, since some members of society (children, the elderly, the infirm) do not and cannot work, meaning that equal provision for them will diminish the proceeds of others. One form of equality is in contradiction with another. Equality presupposes an inequality, and this is true whatever distribution measures one chooses. Marx extends his critique of the language of natural right and natural price to an attack on the entire idea of a "fair" or "equal" wage, a foolishness with which communists dangerously confuse themselves. His endorsement of a "certificate" is an acceptance that some degree of this equal inequality will need to be tolerated early on in the process of communism inasmuch as the "birthmarks of the old society from whose womb it emerges" remain.[18] Unlike the Proudhonian or left Ricardian labor monetarists, however, these certificates are not meant to fix problems—on the contrary, they express given problems and are seen as inherently injurious. The chief difference between Marx's remarks and the labor money reformers mentioned earlier is that, here, Marx presupposes a thoroughgoing reconstruction of the economy—he is operating deductively and logically from the definition of a cooperative society: "in a cooperative society based on common ownership of the means of productions, the producers do not exchange their products; just as little does the labor employed here appear as the value of these products, as a material quality possessed by them."[19] What this means is that, by definition, the certificates would not circulate—they would only be used by individual workers (or perhaps groups of workers) to measure the goods they consumed. They would not function as money to regulate the distribution of raw goods and unfinished products between separate productive units, and therefore they could not function as capital.

This is all very important for Marx, because in the fifteen years since he first began serious work on the critique of political economy,

16 Ibid., 83.

17 Ibid.

18 Ibid., 84.

19 Marx and Engels, *Collected Works*, vol. 22, 85.

he has developed his earlier distinctions considerably. In these mature texts, in the published and unpublished drafts of *Capital,* he has come to discern, between abstract labor and concrete labor, between the value of labor power and the value of the product of labor, a positive social form, which is not simply a magnitude, but an impersonal power that comes to seem a "material quality" of the commodities themselves and therefore coordinates and regulates otherwise uncoordinated collective production. He can speak confidently of the capitalist economy as organized by certain "natural laws" that are, in fact, historically produced. The key difference between the schema he critiques in his earlier work and the scenario that he envisions in "Critique of the Gotha Program" is that, in Marx's view, the "law of value" would not obtain, because in this situation money and commodities would not serve as an impersonal power, coordinating otherwise uncoordinated functions through after-the-fact distribution. Where profit, price, and wage function automatically, compelling the actions of capitalists and laborers, Marx imagines instead conscious decision, free association, deliberate calculation, choice.

The language Marx uses here is nearly identical to the riddling passages in *Capital*, volume 1, on the "fetishism of commodities," which "conceals the social character of private labor and the social relations between workers, by making those relations appear as relations between material objects, instead of revealing them plainly."[20] The two passages are even more deeply connected, as this section of *Capital* is, along with the "Critique of the Gotha Program," among the handful of places in his late writing where Marx discusses communism directly. The mystifications of capitalism, the "magic and necromancy that surrounds the products of labor," can be made visible only by way of contrast with "other forms of production" including an "association of free men." It is in the light of these other social arrangements that we see not only the historical specificity of capitalism but the specific horizon of its overcoming by communism.

In both texts the test of value requires speculation and imagination, not only analytical acuity: "Let us finally imagine, for a change, an association of free men, working with the means of

20 Marx, *Capital*, vol. 1, 168.

production held in common."[21] This is the sentence Penguin put on the back of my tattered copy of the first volume of *Capital*, choosing to excerpt a moment in the text where speculation about communism is recruited in order to highlight elements of capitalism, but the speculative relationship can work the other way, too, as Marx shows in "Critique of the Gotha Program." The test of value is something other than historical narration, however—Marx doesn't show us the historical particularity of the capitalist mode of production by putting it in historical sequence. Rather, he offers a series of analytical distinctions, asking us to consider "forms" of production, but not modes (*Produktionsformen* not *Produktionsweisen*), the first of which, "Robinson on his island," is entirely synthetic, drawn from the pages of bourgeois fiction and chosen to mark a contrast with the "magic and necromancy that surrounds the products of labor on the basis of capitalist production." *Robinson Crusoe* is bourgeois economics as it sees itself and as it sees man: self-knowing and self-possessing, able to record his actions with his diary and his timepiece and to measure the products thereof precisely. But Marx also makes clear that relations can be transparent without being tractable, as in "medieval Europe," where "we find everyone dependent" but where the products of labor are quite transparently distributed among lord and vassal. The same transparency holds in "household production," where labor is organized and wealth distributed according to an organic and transparent division of labor in which individuals are not free but bound to their location. Only in a "form" of production that is synthetic, like "Robinson on his island," but made real by history, do we find "free men, working with means of production held in common and expending their different forms of labour-power in *full self-awareness as one single social labour force*" (italics mine). These distinctions are important because they mean that one might abolish the law of value and its impersonal domination without at the same time abolishing dependency and domination. Only with "free association" do transparency and tractability, self-consciousness and self-activity, coincide. As he emphasizes later, "the veil is not removed from the countenance of the social life-process, i.e., the process of material production, until

---

21 Ibid., 171.

it becomes production by freely associated men and stands under their conscious and planned control."

These passages are essential to illuminating Marx's thinking in his brief remarks in the "Critique of the Gotha Program," and understanding what's at stake when he suggests that in free association labor no longer appears as a property of things. These passages also illuminate that for Marx the utility of value-analysis has remained political through and through. The problem, however, as should be clear from Marx's speculative analysis, is that the abolition of the law of value is not identical to free association. There are forms of heteronomy beyond the law of value—pre-capitalist history testifies to thousands of years of such forms—and though capitalism is the only form we know of in which such heteronomy takes shape as impersonal domination, we cannot rule out the possibility of a non-capitalist or perhaps post-capitalist impersonal domination, a naturalized social law that operates through means other than value but is nonetheless regulative and reproductive of class society. Abolition of the law of value leaves a remainder, and it is from and against this remainder that communism must be made.

A corollary point is that Marx could be wrong here, but for the right reasons. If the form of production employing labor certificates were neither transparent nor tractable, and if furthermore impersonal forms of domination still persisted in such a state of affairs, it would fail if not the negative test of value, then the positive test of communism. Here, though, as Marx affirms in each of the texts quoted, no determination can be made through an examination of distribution alone. The very concept of distribution implies that products are distributed to consumers *post festum*, after production decisions have been made. But the dimension of freedom concerns both ex post and ex ante decision, not just what people consume but what kinds of activities they will perform, and under what conditions. It is the organization of the entirety of social production that is far more significant. If I freely engage in collective production with others, based on my own free intention, and use a piece of paper to ensure that I do not consume so much that others suffer, this is no matter at all. But if that piece of paper is expected, all on its own, to force me to do something I would not otherwise do, then we have a serious problem. This is why Marx insists that the certificate is in fact a superficial technical concern, subordinate to the underlying organization of the economy.

The Test of Value 3: Marx and the GIK

The most serious attempt to flesh out the ideas in the "Critique of the Gotha Program" was conducted by Jan Appel, as a synthesis of his experience of the German Revolution and his attempt to develop the revolutionary example of the workers' council. He and the other members of Group of International Communists (GIK) worked up these insights into *The Fundamental Principles of Communist Production and Distribution*. At the center of Appel's investigation is Marx's labor certificate and a continuous pricing of all consumer goods in terms of the "average social hour of labor," here become, for the council communists, not an instrument of mystification, as in capitalism, but of clarification—a simple heuristic whereby workers can understand their relation to each other, "a plain and intelligible image" whereby "the process of production is laid open to anybody's views."[22] In the GIK council system, workers are paid according to their actual (real-time) hours worked, but goods are distributed according to their average production time. For one hour of work, one receives goods worth an "average social hour of labor." Like Marx, the authors recognize that it is impossible to return to each worker the "undiminished proceeds of [their] labor." Before distribution for individual consumption can occur, numerous deductions from the total social product must be made: for the needs of those who cannot work, such as the infirm, the elderly, and children, for general social goods such as hospitals, schools, and libraries that are provided free of charge, for the work of administration and distribution, and finally for whatever expansion of total or per capita production need be undertaken, if any. If the remaining product is distributed equally to workers, according to time worked, regardless of productivity, then the ratio of all these deductions to the total product determines, reciprocally, a "factor of individual consumption [FIC]"—that is, the fraction of an average

22 Pannekoek, *Workers' Councils*, 26–7.

hour of social product which workers receive for every real-time hour worked. If 20 percent or one-fifth of the total social product is deducted for these general costs, then the FIC is four-fifths, meaning at the end of a forty-hour week the worker will receive labor certificates for thirty-two hours of average social labor. They will be able to consume goods that took, on average, thirty-two hours to produce. Implicitly, the workers consume these extra eight hours as well (or will, eventually), but they do so collectively, rather than individually.

This gap turns out to be the source of a novel invention, unique to the *Grundprinzipien*. Where the GIK document is original, and departs from Marx, is that the necessity of these deductions allows the authors to introduce an important distinction, between "productive establishments" and "establishments for general social use [GSU establishments]." The former produce goods for distribution via labor certificates as well as the means of production which those goods require: food and clothing, iron and cotton. The latter produce goods that are distributed freely, to any and all who need them: education, health care, administration. Productive establishments must, of course, direct some portion of their output to support GSU establishments, and as such the divisions between the two types of establishment and their eventual use does not line up with output neatly. Furthermore, workers in both types of establishment are compensated in labor certificates for time worked. The output of GSU establishments counts, then, only inasmuch as it decreases the FIC. This output, which includes all the goods these establishments consume as well as the consumption of their workers, is paid for by everyone rather than individually, and thus counts as a free gift. Eventually, according to the *Grundprinzipien,* as productivity increases, food, housing, clothing, transportation, and other basic goods and services can be distributed freely and upon request rather than in exchange for labor certificates. As more and more branches of production convert to GSU production, the FIC falls, and the system of council communism moves toward a transcendence of labor certificates. The authors of the *Grundprinzipien* seem to think that free access and completely unmetered distribution is a limit which the asymptotic curve of productive development over time never quite reaches, since the production of specialty items that only a few workers desire can never be done on a GSU basis. Thus, as the system matures and stabilizes, certificates will remain in use for some small portion of special needs, while the majority of what workers consume will be available on demand and without restriction. The *Grundprinzipien* therefore takes very seriously Marx's claim that the certificate is only a transitional state of affairs.

Appel claims not to have read the "Critique of the Gotha Program" until he was preparing the manuscript for publication. Nevertheless, he was able to derive all the features of Marx's writing on labor certificates from a careful reading of the Crusoe passage in *Capital*, volume 1, and other such moments. The GIK text is remarkable in that uniquely among contemporaries it underlines the crucial connection between transparency and tractability in Marx's account of planned economy and also understands that at stake is the concept of value, which the GIK authors insist does not obtain in their schema, since the exchange ratios between two commodities are not expressed in terms of yet a third commodity, but are rather expressed directly. Appel and his co-authors understand that for Marx the law of value is a structure of heteronomy, "a system which raises itself as an alien force over producers," compelling action. In the system they propose, on the other hand, "in a society in which the relations of the producers to the product is directly expressed," this danger does not exist. Anton Pannekoek articulates well why value as such does not obtain in the GIK scheme:

> In a society where the goods are produced directly for consumption there is no market to exchange them; and no value, as expression of the labor contained in them establishes itself automatically out of the processes of buying and selling. Here the labor spent must be expressed in a direct way by the number of hours. The administration keeps book [records] of the hours of labor contained in every piece or unit quantity of product, as well as of the hours spent by each of the workers. In the averages over all the workers of a factory, and finally, over all the factories of the same category, the personal differences are smoothed out and the personal results are intercompared.[23]

23 Ibid., 27.

The key difference here is that the determination of prices does not take place automatically and invisibly. It is not effected through the "lawful" behavior of the market but rather through the decisions of workers and consumers, actions which can change the relevant numerical values. The process does not take place unconsciously behind the backs of the workers but consciously, through a transparent process of collective accounting. The workers' councils are, at root, a system of open books.

The Test of Value 4: Bordiga against the GIK

As fascism, Stalinism, and liberal capitalism vied for control of Europe and the world, the story of the Dutch and German communist left, who refused to join the popular front, was largely forgotten. The documents of the Dutch-German left receive greater scrutiny by French-language publications in the 1930s, chiefly due to the presence of Italian left communists in Belgium and France. Exiled from Italy by Mussolini after 1926, communist workers associated with Amadeo Bordiga and the left faction of the Communist Party of Italy (the Sinistra Italiana), settled in Belgium and France, producing a number of journals in French, among them *Bilan*. Although the Sinistra Italiana, barred from Italy until 1943, is sometime diametrically opposed to the Dutch-German left in its interpretation of the world revolution of 1917, remaining fundamentally faithful to the theses of Lenin's *State and Revolution*, the two positions are brought into contact by virtue of their shared critique of the Soviet Union as state capitalist, a position held by few other Marxist groups at the time.

To recall, sent back to Moscow on behalf of the KAPD in 1921, and traveling by legal non-piratical means, Jan Appel reiterated the party's principled opposition to all work with trade unions or participation in elections. The trade unions and the SPD are the product, Appel tells the Comintern, of the nineteenth-century workers' movement, which hoped to improve the position of workers within capitalism, not abolish it. One therefore selects representatives who know how to operate in parliament and negotiate with the bourgeoisie but who are ill-equipped to conduct a revolution.

The emergence of the workers' council, which has the capacity to organize the entirety of the working class and allow it to participate directly in the revolution, obviates these antiquated mechanisms. The role of the party must be to assist the transition to council power, not negotiate or temporize.

Amadeo Bordiga is likewise intransigent, maximalist, and committed to immediate revolutionary action. But because of the peculiarity of the revolutionary wave in Italy, readers will remember, Bordiga comes to associate the workers' councils with mutualism, syndicalism, and cooperativism, not recognizing the genuinely communist character of conciliar power. Bordiga drew from this experience that what the workers' movement lacked was not conciliar power but intransigent, revolutionary leadership in the party. Once the Communist Party of Italy formed, Bordiga's left faction would retain numerical majority until 1923, but eventually, once the Comintern switched to the policies of the United Front, Antonio Gramsci's *L'ordine nuovo*, oriented to the trade unions and antifascism, became dominant. Because of Gramsci's support for the factory councils in Turin, which he saw as the immediate basis for workers' self-management, Bordiga always associated the position of the KAPD and council communism in general with Antonio Gramsci's factoryism, which was, in fact, much closer to revolutionary syndicalism in its vision of transition to socialism.

After 1926, once Mussolini's power is cemented, Bordiga is first imprisoned and then, when released, leaves politics altogether, refusing even to discuss class struggle with his former comrades. His associates in the Italian left, exiled to France and Belgium, are forced to carry on without him. Bordiga's politics are relentlessly antipersonal; he is committed to leadership by doctrine, not individuals, and rarely signs his texts, giving those he worked with a freedom to carry on as before but also to diverge from Bordiga's sometimes dogmatically held positions. These Italian left-communists-in-exile make contact with other groups expelled from the Comintern and, in the journal *Bilan*, produce two reviews of the *Grundprinzipien*, one positive, the other negative, with both authors trying to develop the critique of syndicalism and factoryism which Bordiga had earlier outlined. It is here, in a series of articles written by Jean Melis as Jehan Mitchell, that one can first read the idea—which will have a powerful afterlife and is the inspiration for the concept of the test of value—that the *Grundprinzipien*, contrary to the claims of the authors, in fact retains "value."

> [The authors of the *Grundprinzipien*] note however that "the suppression of the market must be interpreted in the sense that while the market appears to survive under communism, its social content as regards circulation is entirely different: the circulation of products on the basis of labour time is the basis of new social relation" ... But if the market survives (even if its form and basis are different) it can only function on the basis of value. This is what the Dutch internationalists don't seem to see, "subjugated," as they are, to their formulation about "labour time," which in substance is nothing but value itself.[24]

This argument is merely apodictic, an appeal to authority, and not yet a conclusive "test of value" able to account for the dynamics of the system in question. When Bordiga returns to political life after 1945, joining the new left-communist parties that form in Italy, rehabilitating the maxims of the 1920s, he attempts to do just that, developing his early intuitions about the factory councils and the need for party organization into an extensive critique of what he calls "enterprisism," which he asserts subtends not only liberal capitalism and the mixed economy of postwar Italy, but Stalinist Russia (essentially capitalist in Bordiga's view), as well as the proposals of assorted revolutionary syndicalists, Proudhonians, and council communists, whom he amalgamates sloppily.[25] Bordiga never refers to the *Grundprinzipien* or any council communist document by name and seems fundamentally unable to distinguish between the kind of mutualist labor money schemes Marx criticizes (where producer goods are exchanged) and labor-certificate systems, where they only organize consumption. His approach is actually ethical and even metaphysical rather than, for the most

24 "Bilan, the Dutch Left, and the Transition to Communism (ii)," *International Review* 152 (October 2013), available at International Communist Current, en.internationalism.org. The original is Mitchell, "Problèmes de la période de transition," part III, *Bilan* 34 (August–September 1936): 1133–8, available at Antonie Pannekoek Archives, aaap.be.

25 Bordiga, *The Science and Passion of Communism*, 44.

part, the investigation of dynamics that a rigorous test of value would provide, but this is curiously also the source of its strange power. For Bordiga recognizes that communism is as much a matter of principle as history, an ideal object *and* a real movement toward it. From this he develops his curious Marxist metaphysics, claiming that the theory of communism has been invariant since 1848. The communist program was expressed fully and completely by Marx and Engels, and the task of communists is to preserve this theory and defend it from falsifiers and modernizers.

In these powerful postwar essays, where Bordiga develops his theory of the "enterprise-form," he is not offering a historical account, much less a materialist one. The theory of invariance prevents this, in fact. What he is doing is giving an account of contemporary phenomena that allows him to argue deductively from the first principles of communism—from the very definition of communism as the formation of a classless society, the overcoming of the division of labor, and the opposition between town and county. While based on careful observation and research, his writings on Russia, long acknowledged by readers as the very heart of his theory, are oriented less toward accounting for the trajectory of the USSR than they are to measuring it up in the light of communism. Thus, the clearest explication of his views on "council economy" can be found in his most programmatic texts, in particular "Fundamentals of Revolutionary Communism."[26] There he uses the Italian experience to indict council communism as a whole, linking it back to Sorelian syndicalism, Proudhonian mutualism, and other treatments of the problem that retain markets for both consumer and producer goods. For Bordiga, revolution is not a matter of organizational form but program, which allows him to sometimes erroneously assume all organizational or formal questions are superficial. If the task of the revolution is to abolish classes, to overcome the division of labor and the separation between town and country, then the formation of councils and other self-organizing bodies will not be sufficient to the task, for they will merely follow the grooves laid down by the market. Bordiga is programmatically opposed to any "cell-based" or

26 Amadeo Bordiga, "The Fundamentals of Revolutionary Communism," *Il Programma Comunista* nos 13–15 (1957), available at marxists.org.

"parcel" approach to economy because, in his view (and here I am reconstructing for Bordiga as argument what he presents as dogma) they retain the antagonistic interests among workers positioned in different social locations. Bordiga imagines these interests playing out through a crypto-market which, as Marx has already established in the *Grundrisse* and *A Contribution to the Critique of Political Economy*, would eventually restore to money its power to regulate production according to the law of value. Where there are enterprises, then, Bordiga claims (falsely) there must be a market, "since a measuring system of such complexity couldn't operate without the age-old expedient of a general equivalent, in a word, money, the logical measure of every exchange." The only way to overcome this inner tendency toward the market, and fragmentation into enterprises, is for the party to radically unify the cellular interests of proletarians, doing away with the individual as the locus of decision, and bringing the entire society into unitary construction:

> In socialist society, individuals will not be free to make choices regarding what productive activities they take part in, and what they consume, as both these spheres will be dictated by society, and in the interests of society. By whom? This the inevitable imbecilic question, to which we unhesitatingly reply: in the initial phase it will be the "dictatorship" of the revolutionary proletarian class, whose only organ capable of arriving at a prior understanding of the forces which will then come into play is the revolutionary Party; in a second historical phase, society as a whole will exert its will spontaneously through a diffused economy which will have abolished both the autonomy of classes and of individual persons, in all fields of human activity.

This radically anti-individual anthropology, ungrounded in any account of workers' self-activity, turns out to find its justification in a remarkably novel reading of the "Critique of the Gotha Program," in which Bordiga locates none of the contradictions which have worried us so far:

> No longer can anything be acquired by an individual and bound to his person, or his family, by monetary means: a non-accumulable voucher of a short validity gives him exclusively the right to products for human

> consumption within a still restricted and socially calculated limit. Our conception of the dictatorship (initially; followed by a social, species rationality) over consumption implies that the voucher will not be marked as a certain denomination of money (which one could then convert, for example, all into tobacco or alcohol, rather than into milk or bread), but of specific products, just like the wartime "ration cards."

By specifying not just the quantity of consumption goods but their type, many of the problems raised by the labor certificate question are mooted, since all planning can then take place ex ante. But what has happened to "conscious and planned control" and "free association"?[27] Bordiga's anti-individual reconstruction of the invariant doctrine of communism must ignore Marx's nearly continuous description of communism as "the realm of freedom," organized by "free association" and in which "the free development of each is the condition for the free development of all."[28] If by "party" Bordiga means a central administrative layer, determining what people do and consume in advance, without consultation, then there is no freedom at all, and instead we have the forced collectivism Marx and Engels, in a review of Sergey Nechayev's "Fundamentals of the Future Social System," once called "barracks-room communism."[29] But "party" might also mean only the collective locus of decisions taking into account both production constraints and consumption demands—for example, a collective canteen that, surveying local needs and desires, orders ingredients and develops a menu.

Bordiga's lucent statement of the tasks of communism does raise important challenges to the GIK's *Grundprinzipien*, indicating at the very least that the system of proletarian locations, obligations, and

---

27 The treatment of these topics in *The German Ideology*, which in particular Bordiga to his own discredit notes is the fullest articulation of communism that Marx ever produced, contradicts Bordiga's interpretation in several places. "Only within the community has each individual the means of cultivating his gifts in all directions; hence personal freedom becomes possible only within the community ... In the real community the individuals obtain their freedom in and through their association." Marx and Engels, *Collected Works*, vol. 5, 78.

28 Karl Marx and Friedrich Engels, *Collected Works*, vol. 6 (London: Lawrence & Wishart, 1994), 506; Karl Marx, *Capital*, vol. 3 (New York: Penguin, 1991), 958.

29 Marx and Engels, *Collected Works*, vol. 23, 543.

rights introduced by a conciliar society would need to be dynamic, and not simply reproduce the technical division of labor left to it by capitalism, lest it fail to achieve the fundamental objectives of emancipation. Bordiga is vague, however, about the precise mechanisms of the alternative, about what he means by "party," inasmuch as his insistence on invariant theory, on the content rather than the form of communism, comes down in the end to a blind faith that the party, as extension of doctrine, applying Marxian logical operators to matters of necessity, will simply figure it out when the time comes. The party for Bordiga is something of a black box, an empty locus of decision-making, a form which is a content and therefore curiously undetermined. This means, perhaps, that we can swap in more concrete structures, ones predicated on free self-activity, where Bordiga has not.

Though Bordiga does, in these essays, warn that the fragmentation of conciliar economy will necessarily require the reassertion of the law of value, for the most part he does not provide us with a "test of value," but with something else, something just as useful: a "test of communism," an evaluation of conciliar economy from the standpoint of classless, moneyless, stateless society. Sometimes he argues from the particular determinants of capitalism—money, commodity, market, profit—and in finding these, finds that capitalism persists. But for the most part, instead he examines various programs or concrete instantiations of socialism in light of the definition of communism, of classless society, given by Marx and Engels, and finds them wanting. One of my primary objectives in this essay is to demonstrate that the test of value is not the test of communism and that the confusion between the two fundamentally occludes the tasks of communism. There is a gap between the two tests, and the power of Bordiga's critique is not, as it imagines, that it locates value in these various post-capitalist scenarios but that it formulates what must be done *to produce communism* once and as value has been abolished. Both Appel and Bordiga confuse the two tests, with Appel concluding that because his scenario has passed the test of value it has therefore passed the test of communism, and Bordiga concluding that because it has not passed the test of communism it has therefore not passed the test of value. Even if we do not agree with Bordiga that a council revolution would have been doomed for its abjuring of the crucial role of the party, we can agree with him that there are particular tasks that will need to be accomplished by that system if it will pass into communism, and these tasks might be occluded or even hindered by the council system as it emerges from the mass strike. The council revolution would need to overcome the division of labor between enterprises, reorganize the relationship between town and country, and avoid being resubordinated by the nation-state and, in turn, the international market system. It would have to make production decisions ex ante and not simply distribution decisions ex post, and therefore neither associations of producers nor associations of consumers could be the locus of power, but rather both production and consumption decisions must be made synthetically, something that distribution through the workplace by labor certificate or wage prohibits, inasmuch as it splits producers from consumers and makes the former the rights bearer of the latter. Communism requires the overcoming of this gap, which the certificate merely papers over.

Bordiga's critique would be little known if it were not for the interest taken in it by French communists in the 1960s, particularly Jacques Camatte and Gilles Dauvé, whose innovative attempt to come to terms with the revolutionary wave of 1968 built powerfully upon Bordiga's writing on Russia and his critique of the council form. Gilles Dauvé's formulation of revolution as a process of communization, the immediate production of communist relations, essentially follows from a critical synthesis of the theory of council communism with that of the Italian communist left, preserving Appel's emphasis on self-organization, on conscious and planned control, but arguing through Bordiga that the council communist project would have failed had it followed the lines laid out in the *Grundprinzipien*, inasmuch as it preserved value. Dauvé first developed this critique in an untranslated essay, "Sur l'idéologie ultragauche" (On ultraleft ideology), written for the 1969 meeting of Informations et Correspondances Ouvrières (ICO), then the major council communist group in France.[30] ICO had broken away from the group Socialisme

30 In François Danel, ed., *Rupture dans la théorie de la révolution: Textes 1965–1975* (Geneva: Entremonde, 2018), 205–15.

ou Barbarie (S. ou B.), a frequent object of Bordiga's critical remarks, in the 1950s, and it was in and around S. ou B., formed by dissident Trotskyists after World War II, that part of the revival of council communism in France occurred.[31] But because, for curious historical reasons already discussed, the Italian left also had some representation in the French "ultraleft," the obvious discrepancy between these different visions needed to be investigated. Dauvé summarizes Bordiga's critique thus:

> Rejecting the theory of workers' self-management [of the council communists], Bordigism performs one of the most trenchant critiques of the Russian economy, putting in the forefront not the bureaucracy, as Trotskyists and *Socialisme ou Barbarie* do, but the relations of production. The revolution, insists the Bordigist press, must consist of the destruction of the law of value and exchange.[32]

The influence of this final sentence—which describes communism as the destruction of value—has been enormous and will more or less form the vernacular understanding of the theory of communization developed by Dauvé and those he influences. What is communism? Destruction of value-form. What is the task of revolution as communization? To abolish value.

These formulations have been a powerful tonic for revolutionary communism since 1968, establishing a long-sought-after link between Marx's esoteric theory of value and the tasks of communism. But Dauvé confuses the test of value and the test of communism, thereby weakening his critique. However, if we reformulate as test of communism what Dauvé describes as test of value, we retain the power of his critical formulation of the tasks of communism in light of Marx's theory of value, without confusing value, capitalism, and communism.

---

31 Marcel van der Linden, "Socialisme ou Barbarie: A French Revolutionary Group, 1949–1965," *Left History* 5, no. 1 (1997), available at libcom.org; Henri Simon, "Workers' Inquiry in Socialisme ou Barbarie," trans. Asad Haider and Salar Mohandesi, *Viewpoint Magazine* 3, September 26, 2013, viewpointmag.com.

32 Translation mine. Danel, *Rupture dans la théorie de la révolution*, 214.

Gilles Dauvé's publication history is tortuous, but he has been revising this essay for the past fifty years. English-language readers were introduced to his work with the publication of *Eclipse and Re-emergence of the Communist Movement* in 1974, translated by Fredy Perlman for Black & Red Press, then an important site for the distribution of broadly ultraleft material, Guy Debord's *Society of the Spectacle* in particular.[33] In the book, Dauvé revises "Sur l'idéologie ultragauche" into the chapter "Leninism and the Ultraleft." Dauvé reads "Critique of the Gotha Program" in a manner similar to Bordiga, suggesting that it represents a schema for the distribution of use value *after* the law of value has been destroyed. But Dauvé has a curious, confused understanding of the relationship between the lawfulness of the "law" of value and the measurement of labor time, suggesting that if a labor standard, an average hour of social labor, persists then so, too, does value, an understanding of value that comes dangerously close to confusing it with instrumental rationality as such, since adding up sums and dividing them to find averages need not inherently imply any structure of distribution. Dauvé rightly notes that value analysis, the test of value, must take account of the "dynamics" of a particular system, but because he confuses the law of value with one of its particular functions and presuppositions, the measurement of labor time, what he gives us is not really a dynamical analysis based on the actual material structure of the GIK scheme but an account of how, already latent, the law of value must reassert itself:

> Marx excludes the hypothesis of any gradual way to communism through the progressive destruction of the law of value. On the contrary, the law of value keeps asserting itself violently until the overthrow of capitalism: the law of value never ceases destroying itself—only to reappear at a higher level.

---

33 Jean Barrot (Gilles Dauvé) and François Martin, *Eclipse and Re-emergence of the Communist Movement* (Detroit: Black & Red, 1974). This text has undergone several revisions, and all HTML versions have been edited to reflect changes made to the 2015 PM Press edition. Unless the new version is indicated, page numbers are from the PDF of the 1997 Antagonism Press edition, which reproduces the interior chapters of the 1974 edition: Gilles Dauvé and François Martin, *Eclipse and Re-emergence of the Communist Movement* (London: Antagonism Press, 1997).

> The theory of the management of society through workers' councils does not take the dynamics of capitalism into account. It retains all the categories and characteristics of capitalism: wage-labour, law of value, exchange. The sort of socialism it proposes is nothing other than capitalism—democratically managed by the workers. If this were put into practice there would be two possibilities: either the workers' councils would try not to function as in capitalist enterprises, which would be impossible since capitalist production relations would still exist. In this case, the workers' councils would be destroyed by counter-revolution ... Or the workers' councils would consent to functioning as capitalist enterprises. In this case the system of councils would not survive; it would become an illusion, one of the numerous forms of association between Capital and Labour.[34]

The dynamic analysis works only if we accept his apodictic claim that the law of value is still present. But is it? In the GIK scheme, producer goods are not exchanged but distributed directly between productive units according to calculations that follow from social need first and productive capacity second, unlike in capitalism. In fact, calculation of labor-time prices is not sufficient to distribute products and labor among the different producers, only to calculate the proportions between them, given existing need. In capitalism, such distribution happens because capitalists enter into new lines of production or invest in new plants and machinery in order to achieve higher rates of return—as a second-order consequence, this movement of capital (and labor, since labor follows capital) then meets new social need poorly and only if that social need first meets the requirements of production for profit. In the GIK system, given amounts of final products desired would be determined before the fact, based on a survey of social need. Even if one can be skeptical about how such a survey might function, the point is that output totals for individual units will need to be chosen directly, not determined by the average rate of profit, and this is the most important sense in which the "law" of value is not operating.

Further, in the GIK system, production norms can't be established automatically, behind the backs of producers, as a consequence of the self-interested motives of individual owners or enterprises.

34 Ibid., 73.

When you pay people eight "hours" of social wealth in exchange for any eight hours of actual work, there is no given mechanism for establishing a production norm, and no inherent force compelling workers to a certain level of output. In capitalism, labor power is purchased, and becomes the property of the capitalist during the time of production—capitalists can set any terms they demand, within biological limits and sometimes the bounds of bourgeois law. They can set output norms and fire workers if they don't meet them. But in the GIK system, as in any system that calls itself socialist or communist, labor is an obligation, not a right. If everyone who can work must work, then no one can be dismissed. The GIK system would thus find itself unable to enforce production norms except through an already existing unanimous will or the reintroduction of structures of incentive and political violence. If such unanimity already exists, however, then the certificate is superfluous, a mere bookkeeping instrument.

Furthermore, the GIK system implicitly raises problems of reporting and accounting, since it depends on either honest self-reporting or surveillance. As Marx notes in "Critique of the Gotha Program," in a point reiterated by Bordiga, the fragmentation of production into blocks of producers working with very different tools and capacities, in workplaces of differing sizes, situated in geographically particular locations, means that one can't establish uniform productive norms. Workers in particular units can potentially set their own norms or even lie about their output. They might be compelled to do this if they think the system is unfair. If, for example, the distribution of existing productive capacities makes things harder for some workers and easier for others, they might decide not to follow production norms, bringing themselves into conflict with other producers.

This is where Marx's and Bordiga's remarks about the determinative effect of the underlying organization of production and not the system of distribution are highly apropos. To the extent the GIK system is successful it would have to do away with the fragmented enterprization of production, which leads to a situation where producers in different enterprises have opposed interests. This can happen only by way of a thoroughgoing reorganization of the underlying apparatus, doing away with iniquities baked into the material infrastructure. This is particularly obvious in the case of agriculture, one of Bordiga's primary focuses. The "councilization" of existing agricultural enterprises will obviously be insufficient, even if one did not take as one's immediate task the overcoming of the division between town and country.[35] Even in the US, much agricultural production takes place through small family-owned and -operated farms whose interests are opposed through production for profit. Councilization of these farms will, at the very least, have to involve processes of collectivization and material reorganization largely incompatible with the continuity of family-operated production, even before the problems of the division of town and country are confronted. For Bordiga, the persistence of such market-oriented petty producers in the Soviet Union meant that capitalism had not been abolished, since markets still existed and, as he points out, linked Soviet agriculture to the discipline of international trade, world money, and ultimately, mediation by the law of value, particularly through circulating capital, where international trade remained. We can agree with Bordiga about the external mediation of the Soviet economy by the law of value without thinking value operative and regulative in Russia. With regard to the test of value, Bordiga's analysis has to be judged in terms of not only its categorical claims but the dynamics attributed to the USSR. These dynamics might not be governed by the law of value but nonetheless lead toward its reinstantiation or toward something equally bad. Furthermore, they can be demonstrated to lead away from communism—that is, they fail the test of communism. Dynamical analysis can be conducted for a system, even a non-capitalist one, inasmuch as it is shown to possess capacity for unintended development. The point is to show not only what it is but where it's going, and, in this sense, even if Bordiga gets the nouns wrong, he gets the verbs right.

The Demon in the Matrix

Up until 1997, Gilles Dauvé revises *Eclipse and Re-emergence of the Communist Movement*, by adding new prefaces, introductions, or appendices. The 2015 PM Press addition features substantial interior revisions, however, and the chapter "Leninism and the Ultraleft,"

35 Bordiga, *The Science and Passion of Communism*, 426–60.

which we have been tracking, has now been split into three chapters, one of which, "Value, Time, and Communism: Rereading Marx," clarifies his earlier remarks on value:

> For the GIK, the company explicitly stood as an economic unit at the centre of the system. Of course, council communists were aware of the inescapable fact that some companies, and some workers within each company, would be more productive than others: they thought this would be compensated for by a complex regulating mechanism detailed by Mattick. However, if the regulator is labour time, this entails the imperative of being productive, and productivity is no servant: it rules over production. The shop floor would soon lose control over its elected supervisors, and democratically designated co-organisers would act as bosses. The system of councils would survive as an illusion, and workers' management result in capitalism, or rather … capitalism would never have disappeared. We can't have it both ways: either we keep the foundation of value, or we dispense with it. The circle can't be squared.
>
> Such a scheme goes as close as one can get to keeping the essentials of capitalism yet putting them under full worker control.[36]

This is an improvement but still confuses the test of value with the test of communism. My point here is not to refute Dauvé's critique, which I think accurately diagnoses some of the dynamic trajectories of the GIK system, but to criticize it sympathetically and better identify the offending elements, disentangling test of value from test of communism.

Dauvé still confuses conscious *measurement of* labor time with *regulation by* labor time. These must be distinguished. Imagine, as reductio assumption, a society of pure abundance in which people spend only a few hours each day interacting with nature and their

36 Dauvé and Martin, *Eclipse and Re-emergence of the Communist Movement*, 120. It is not clear what prompted such a massive revision, but these parts of the book received a very illuminating response in David Adam, "Marx's Critique of Socialist Labor-Money Schemes and the Myth of Council Communism's Proudhonism," libcom.org, January 23, 2013. Adam importantly distinguishes between labor money, as criticized in the early texts, and labor certificates, a distinction that neither Bordiga nor Dauvé seems to register. The authors respond to Adam in a note in the PM Press version.

tools in order to generate resources far in excess of their needs. There is no metering of social wealth. People simply take what they need, with or without prior arrangement. Decisions about production are made ex ante, with an eye to social need. What effect would the *measurement* of average labor time—how many hours it takes to make a pair of shoes, on average—have in such a system? It would certainly not, on its own, affect the distribution of wealth or be able to direct people to certain activities over others. It would be no different, in this way, than calculating the average height or weight of the nine-year-olds in a town or counting how many people you needed to harvest a given field. Useless? Perhaps. Dangerous? Not inherently, not unless you think the practice of addition leads inexorably to the value-form.

The danger lies not in measurement itself, as if the tools of abstract mathematical analysis contained, encrypted in their depths, the necessary conditions for the value-form: *where goes calculus, there must follow capital.* No, the danger lies in the regulative effect of labor-time measurement, a regulation that occurs not only through measurement but through the certification and individualization of access to social wealth (which requires measurement as its condition). Money, we must remember, has particular functions: measure of value, medium of exchange, means of payment, store of value. Some functions are subordinate to others. For example, the function of medium of exchange presupposes that money is measure of value, but it does not work the other way. Measuring does not presuppose the function of medium of exchange, store of value, and means of payment, let alone capital. The test of value asks us to examine the labor certificate precisely in light of these functions and to note that it comes up short—in other words, the key problem with the certificate is not that it can regulate production as money does but that it can't, and that it will then either break down or necessitate further mechanisms that amount to the reinstation of value and the transformation of the labor certificates back into money and money wages. The logical disjunction, the either-or, can't be avoided here, since at stake are matters of free political action in the face of obstacles.

To be specific about the gap, note that Dauvé says that, instead of the freely associated workers measuring value, measurement will, in turn, control their actions. But how could this happen? It could happen only if the certificate, in addition to guaranteeing a certain amount of products, also *forced* a certain level of labor. But as written, there is no way for the certificate to do so. Any eight hours, no matter what the person does, counts for access to eight hours of social wealth. There is no way to establish a productivity norm by means of the labor certificate alone, unless one imagines workers can be dismissed. But in the GIK system, unemployed people also have access to social wealth, so this is no solution. There would be no way to force a production norm on a particular enterprise. Some other mechanism would be required—sanction, incentive, direct violence—independent of the certificate. The problem is then not only what the certificate does but what it doesn't do. The certificate does not allow the workers to freely regulate production, but neither does it automatically push them around from workplace to workplace while establishing production norms. That will require political structures of communication, or mechanisms of control, which themselves must be judged not only by the test of value but by the test of communism.

Bordiga and Dauvé suggest the producers will have to liberalize the certificate, allowing it to function like money, to reward enterprises and individuals differently according to different output. But one could also imagine that the system would simply break down. If it didn't, if the system were able to regulate production with the certificate, then this would mean that the certificates were simply unnecessary as regulating mechanism. There is no dynamic justification for them. This makes the implications of the test of value a bit different than construed. It is not the argument from necessity that Bordiga and Dauvé suppose—it is not that the labor certificate, or measurement of labor time, will *of necessity* lead back to value, to capitalism, as a slice of potato will, when submerged, transform into a whole plant. Marx sometimes argues from necessity, as with the labor money which will necessarily turn into money as such. But he also argues by logical disjunction, when he suggests that, in order to achieve its aims (i.e., to obviate the conditions for the necessary reintroduction of money as such), either labor money would require a despotic, totally administered planner state, or it would simply be unnecessary, as a solution to problems that free association and free development have already overcome.

The danger, then, is not that the GIK system will become a self-managed capitalism, as is sometimes supposed—that could happen only by replacing the certificates with real money. The danger is that, inasmuch as the labor certificate can't do what it is supposed to do, other social relations will. The failure of the system then looks closer to the actual course of the USSR, which failed not because it continued capitalist accumulation but because it could not. The USSR was, in the words of Chris Arthur, a "clock without a spring"—it retained the underlying infrastructure of capitalism but lacked the social relations necessary to effectively distribute goods and workers in a way that drove balanced growth.[37] The failures of the system then derive from the responses of the state, planners, and managers to such a state of affairs, which constituted attempts to manually advance the clockworks of value through forms of direct violence. The law of value did not operate in the USSR except through a form of political mimesis.

Therefore, if we want to call labor-time measurement "value," then we must admit that such value is only ideal, has not been made regulative, and does not function automatically behind the backs of producers, determining both production and investment decisions after the fact. I think this use of terminology is confused and would propose that, following Marx, we distinguish between *abstract labor* and value, where abstract labor is an essential part of value but where it might exist without the lawfulness of value being in operation. For abstract labor is closer to the element of measure that Dauvé wants to make identical with the value-form. Abstract labor brings two entirely dissimilar, commodified acts of labor together and represents their content in a third commodity, the money commodity. It creates equality across inequality, of a sort that, as Marx insists, still persists in the labor-certificate scheme. Value, in contrast to abstract labor, is when the magnitudes of abstract labor come to seem a property of things themselves, and where these properties, on their own, compel the decisions of workers and capitalists. If I work eight hours making shoes, produce six pairs of shoes, and receive six hours of social wealth, but my friend Joshua makes eight pairs of shoes in his

37 Christopher Arthur, "Epitaph for the USSR: A Clock without a Spring," *Critique* 30, no. 1 (2002): 91–122.

workplace, also receiving six hours of social wealth, then we have something similar to abstract labor occurring, in which the mass of products corresponding to six hours of social wealth comes to represent the content of two entirely dissimilar acts of labor. This is what Marx is thinking about when he refers to the persistence of bourgeois right, an abstract equality that can be mapped only across existing inequalities. It is not clear that abstract labor can be said to exist, however, if there are no regulative mechanisms to enforce it. Best to think of it as a kind of potentiality, a demon trapped within the matrix of the system. Needless to say, any attempt to make it regulative, to release the demon, whether through blockchain or Lagrangian measures of opportunity cost, would just be the return of value, making itself adequate to all the functions of money.

No such mechanisms exist in the GIK system, not even potentially, and so one can't even surmise a direct trajectory toward the reimposition of value. The higher productivity of Joshua does not let his enterprise undersell me or attract more capital for its higher profit rate. In capitalism, with value, the presence of the unequal equality across the two producers sets in motion dynamic interactions which force a general increase in productivity and shift labor and capital from one enterprise to another. Nothing of the sort happens in Marx's or the GIK's system. If the workers' councils want, in response to this discrepancy, to raise my productivity, this will have to be done through political decision and direct distribution. There is nothing in the system that can force me to work harder. If one wants to force things, one will need force.

The Test of Communism

"Sur l'ideologie ultragauche," the article which introduces the test of value to English-language readers, had as its intended audience the 1969 meeting of Informations et Correspondances Ouvrières, to which participants from across the world had been invited.[38] Dauvé and François Martin had come to reconsider the ideology of workers' self-management that dominated the centers of ultraleft

38 Danel, *Rupture dans la théorie de la révolution*, 205–15.

activity during the events of May 1968. In their first revision, they preface the article by saying they had hoped to engage Paul Mattick in conversation—a logical choice, given his prominence then as one of the chief exponents of council communism, and a rather open-minded and intellectually curious one. The term they use, *ultragauche*, is a new one, meant to encompass the broad sweep of groups aligned with but by no means derivable from historical council communism. In France, ICO was the most prominent of such groups.

What is fascinating, and what has gone largely unremarked on, is that by 1969 Paul Mattick had revised his earlier position on the *Grundprinzipien* and no longer considered the labor certificate necessary or practicable, given the transformation of capitalism since the 1930s.[39] Indeed, when Mattick writes an introduction to the 1970 republication of the *Grundprinzipien* in German, his mature assessment is rather withering and if not more total certainly more precise than Dauvé's. For one, he notes that the productive forces have developed so that, in most of the world, the point has long been passed where most goods could be put directly into the GSU category. But even if this were not the case, perhaps because of destruction of the productive forces by class struggle, he finds the certificate "superfluous" in every case he can imagine. Where there is scarcity, freely associated producers can simply ration consumption without distributing through the workplace, and in such a way that labor-time calculation for purposes of distribution is unnecessary. Even when it comes to the organization of production and the distribution of goods between productive units, Mattick finds labor-time calculation of limited utility and rues the fact that the authors spend so little time discussing the much more fundamental question of how given levels of need will be determined.

After such critique, very little is left standing. Why then introduce the book at all, since its most basic techniques are judged impertinent? For Mattick, it seems, the devil is not actually in the details—rather, the text is an exposition of the idea that the economy

39 Paul Mattick, "Introduction to *Grundprinzipien kommunistischer Produktion und Verteilung*," trans. Jac. Johanson, *Controversies: Forum for the International Communist Left*, July 26, 2014, leftcommunism.org.

might be brought under "conscious and planned control." The chief criticism of the ultraleft that Dauvé raises is that it is purely formalist, that it fails to define the *content* of communism and instead confuses it with political autonomy and self-management, which are merely political forms. But Mattick, if you read his introduction closely, rejects the particular forms elaborated by the GIK and in fact offers for examination its content, classless society, which he defines as workers' autonomy and the abolition of exploitation. The details, in other words, will have to be adjusted to accord with these principles, and if one believes that the workers can manage production, then certainly they can amend the details of the GIK proposal as necessary.

Paul Mattick was only twenty-two when Jan Appel began writing the *Grundprinzipien*. An active youth participant in the communist left, Mattick and others had actually been planning to break Appel out of jail in Dusseldorf, but called off the plan when Appel was offered a lesser sentence.[40] Fifty years later, living in the United States, Mattick is particularly well-positioned to see the *Grundprinzipien* as a historical document, its vision conforming to the position of the working class circa World War I. This was perhaps the largest, best-organized working class in the history of the workers' movement, poised to seize control of the industrial heartlands of Western Europe. Was such a vision doomed, even then? It does not seem possible to derive such a conclusion, once we dispense with the idea that value is latent within the GIK proposal. Inarguably, attempts to simply councilize existing production would have run into powerful obstacles, especially if the certificate was meant to force production norms. But imagine a modified GIK proposal in which basic goods (food, housing, health care) were immediately placed in the GSU category. If most of the industries producing such goods could be run by the council system, then this might allow ample time for the reorganization of production in order to overcome the conflicts produced by the division of labor and the prior distribution of fixed means of production. The GIK proposal makes sense for an industrializing country with a growing working class organized in large units and capable of quickly delivering basics, such as existed in much of

40 Gary Roth, *Marxism in a Lost Century: A Biography of Paul Mattick* (Chicago: Haymarket, 2016), 45.

the world during the midcentury. But after deindustrialization, as Mattick indicates, such a proposal looks very different.

In light of the test of communism, then, the formal mechanisms are not determinative. What matters is whether the form is compatible with communism. What is communism? We have already encountered some definitions: classless, moneyless, stateless society; freely associated workers meeting their needs with the means of production under conscious and planned control. Communism is prismatic, and therefore either of these definitions is sufficient and interchangeable. If there is a class, a state, or money, then there cannot be conscious or planned control. But by the same measure, if a piece of paper like the certificate does not inhibit conscious and planned control, then it is not money.

Imagine, for example, a state of affairs in which freely associated laborers work, voluntarily, in a number of different workshops according to a common plan. If there is no compulsion to work, if the activity is freely chosen, and if those who can't or won't work don't need to, then a certificate used to portion receipts is not a mechanism of compulsion at all; it is bookkeeping, and serves simply to ration social wealth according to a plan likewise equally chosen. It may be unnecessary or trifling, but it certainly is not dangerous. Under such a state of affairs, there is no difference between the certificate and a simple voluntary record of individual withdrawal from the stores of social wealth. It is a recording instrument and nothing more, less like money than a ledger in which one records one's receipts or a chore wheel in a collective house. But then at the very least we might say that the labor certificate, if it is still called so, truly misnames itself, for it is not a piece of paper exchanged for labor but simply a mechanism whereby society divides available wealth among its members. This is the only way in which the certificate might be demystified, rendered transparent: when it becomes simply a consumption token.

Here we come upon the difference between what Evgeny Pashukanis calls legal regulation of society and technical regulation.[41] The very concepts of law and right, argues Pashukanis, presuppose as their abstract basis a "legal subject," the bearer of rights. One sees

41 Evgeny B. Pashukanis, Barbara Einhorn, and Chris Arthur, *Law and Marxism: A General Theory* (London: Pluto, 1990), 81.

clearly how the certificate presupposes such a subject, and in fact Pashukanis's theory of law is derived from a novel reading of "Critique of the Gotha Program," underscoring that Marx identifies the certificate and the forms of equalized inequality they presuppose with "bourgeois right," that birth defect preserved in socialism. For Pashukanis, legal regulation through the determination of the rights of abstract subjects emerges as the particular consequence of the equal inequality of exchange relations, which both civil and criminal law reproduces in abstracted form. What bourgeois right presupposes is that exchange takes place between individuals with conflicting interests, for only then is it required that the state enforce contracts and resolve disputes. To draw out the basis of the legal subject in conflicting interests, Pashukanis compares legal regulation, in which some body imbued with the power to settle dispute by implicit violence forces contracts upon one or more legal subjects, with the situation of technical regulation, where an underlying commonality of interest leads to a common rule. For example, the liability of a railway owner for consigned freight is an order of regulation different from a timetable which ensures trains do not crash into each other. In the first, there are competing interests, in the second there aren't. Likewise, a situation where a labor certificate forces someone who does not want to work to labor by linking abstract responsibility (to work) to abstract right (to consume) is entirely different from a situation in which a labor certificate is simply used to portion the distribution of social wealth among freely associated volunteers. One might even use violence to rectify such a situation—such as forcing a train off the rails if it might produce a crash, without reference to a conflict of interest. Such violence is in the interest of all, even the conductor who is forced off the track.

This underlying arrangement of interest, keyed to a distribution of means of production, is in fact the object of what Bordiga, confusingly, calls the *content of communism*. Bordiga identifies the content of communism with doctrine and theoretical principle rather than historical process and thereby commits an idealist error. Implicit in his analysis, however, is that the conflicting interests sedimented into class division and the division of labor can be overcome only through a process of social reengineering, fusing the broken shards of the scattered means of production into a cohesive whole that presupposes a common plan and common interests. This is in fact the object of the test of communism, for which doctrine or principle can serve merely as revolutionary heuristic. Where latent conflicts of interests between parcelized enterprises thwart commonality of interest and plan, there the work of communism cannot simply apply an abstract form to those interests, hoping to solder them together; it must remake them in their real materiality. To do so, the test of communism in fact draws upon an abstract ideal, the concept of communism, of classless society, which we can read as the negation of those elements not only of capitalism but of class society since the Neolithic revolution: division of labor, state, and class.

The task of the communist revolution, then, is not simply to abolish value, though this is a first act which cannot be skipped over. The law of value is the dynamic inner consistency of the capitalist mode of production, this ravager of worlds. But value binds together other elements, it is the spectral ring which holds together the other rings of market, money, state, law, class, and division of labor. Once value has been destroyed, those other elements might persist, carrying with them ancient forms of heteronomy that might be combined in new forms. Once one destroys the final boss of value, there are still other enemies that must be defeated. The revolution will do so, however, by focusing on the ground which all these other forms presuppose: opposed interests, sedimented into the real material relations between people.

Among the worst aspects of the certificate, then, when pitched against opposed interests, is that it implies a social judgment about the capacity to labor which is implicitly built upon bourgeois notions of the connection between right and labor. The sources of the classical labor theory of value lie in early rationalist theories of property, in particular that of John Locke, who writes, "Whatsoever, then he removes out of the state that Nature hath provided and left in it, he hath mixed his labor with, and joined to it something that is his own, and thereby makes it is his property."[42] The bourgeois ethics of labor and right subtend the workers' movement, as we have seen, and form the primary objects of Marx's first formulation of the test

42 John Locke, *Two Treatises on Civil Government* (London: G. Routledge and Sons, 1884), 204.

of value. It is impossible under capitalism, given joint production, to return to the worker the value they have produced. There is no way to write such a sentence as a logical proposition which is not false on every interpretation. This Lassallean delusion persists in the labor movement; it is written into the bourgeois law regulating strikes and wages, and taken over into certain syndicalist visions that imagine absolute control over each workplace only by those involved. Not only will communism inherit a division of labor requiring a vast commonality of production, but it will have to turn this into a true commonality, on an entirely different basis. Every bit of the earth is now so intermixed and intermingled with so many human labors and forms of indebtedness and belonging that it would be ludicrous to parcel it out and say to whom which belongs. This is easily seen in the problem of climate that will confront any communism we can imagine. The burning of hydrocarbons, the release of carbon from the soil, cannot be the choice of those who work the land alone, since it has consequences for everyone and for all common production. Our labors have taken to the air, and there is no way to put them back into the bottle. The task of communism will be to overcome all egoizing structures and to communize consumption and production, to render visible our common interdependence, in direct, collective provision of basic needs in which decisions about what to generate and what to consume are brought together into conscious planning bodies.

When you certificate food, housing, and other necessities, you create needless individualism, fragmenting consumption. You establish an explicit social judgment about those who can work and those who cannot, those who give their labors and those who take from the social store without contributing (because they are children, disabled, elderly). But who can make such a judgment? And are we sure that these individuals do not contribute to reproduction in ways that are simply unmeasured? If consumption is individualized, there will certainly be forms of unpaid labor, occurring in private spaces of consumption. In capitalism, the division between paid and unpaid labor is gendered, racialized, and ableist. Waged workers receive money, which is used to support the reproduction of unwaged workers, but such that informal structures of interpersonal domination mediate activity. At stake here is not really whether structures like the family persist but whether they are actively enforced in communism, through the social judgment of the labor certificate. Communizing consumption does away with this problem immediately, allowing us to distinguish between forms of kinship and personal relation that are voluntary and those that are not.

It's not only feasible to do that but probably superior, for where consumption is already common, according to common plan, there will interests be fused. If limited personal goods are distributed individually through the workplace, perhaps even as incentive, it does not seem that this would counter the vast commonality of life already established on the basis of voluntary activity and free, collective access, and such individual distribution would likely quickly become anachronistic. How else would it be with so much in common? In this sense, even though the cell form of bourgeois right persisted in some vestigial way it would be much like the wig on an English barrister, not capable of parcelizing individual interest. There would be no "legal regulation" even though some sort of abstract equality persisted, since the underlying plan will have presumed commonality of interest.

The test of communism is a concept, and no concept will ever produce communism, not even the concept of communism. To become more than a concept, the test of communism will need to be reformulated as tasks, by a movement capable of accomplishing it. Such tasks presuppose an understanding of the difference between capitalism and communism, of their mutual incompatibility.

Perhaps one way to formulate the insights of this chapter is to say that the relationship between capitalism and communism is one of non-conjunction rather than disjunction. There can be capitalism. There can be communism. But there cannot be *both* capitalism and communism. Their relationship is not-and, non-conjunction, rather than a simple either-or disjunction. We might formulate this as the axiom of contradiction, for this represents the true contradiction in capitalism between labor and capital, otherwise mutually presupposing aspects of capitalism. The futures which these classes project are in contradiction, even where the classes themselves are not.

Marx develops, refines, and clarifies the test of communism by adding to it, as a presupposition, the test of value—the adequate concept of capitalism. In doing so, he makes clear that the relationship between capitalism and communism is one of non-conjunction, demonstrating the existence of modes of production that are neither capitalist nor communist (or, to see it from the point of view of his contemporaries, he demonstrates that capitalism is a variety of class society, not its general form). To the axiom of contradiction, he adds what we might call the common ruin corollary: there can be neither capitalism nor communism. If you treat the relationship between capitalism and communism as either-or disjunction, you forget other modes of production exist beyond capitalism and communism, and you assume that only communism can emerge from capitalism and that whatever emerges from capitalism which is not communism is therefore simply more capitalism. To be specific, not both capitalism and communism means either not-capitalism or not-communism. What the non-conjunction of capitalism and communism implies is a choice of negations by way of which the positive content of communism is revealed. Either capitalism will be suppressed or communism will.

The test of communism tells us what but not how: it must be armed; it must break the armed power of the state; it must be proletarian, drawing the vast majority of society into voluntary associations laying direct claim to the totality of social wealth; it must be communist, provisioning for common use according to a common plan without legal regulation or exchange; it must overcome the divisions between people and places cemented into the division of labor and the structure of the enterprise; it must be transparent, comprehensible to all, and tractable, allowing people to participate in decisions that concern them through structures of recallable, mandated delegation committed to the reproduction of classless, moneyless, stateless society.

3
Inquiry, Organization, and the Long 1968

Because they hail from the future, the workers' councils are easily lost to history, betrayed by official histories of the revolution and its actors. As coherent theory, practice, and history, council communism is largely a reconstruction after the fact, developed in the 1930s, kept alive through the 1940s and finding new adherents after World War II. But it was only with the New Left, in the US and Western Europe, that real interest emerged. Much of the historiography this study relies on originates in this moment, which, in the words of Axel Weipert, "popularized the council movement as an anti-authoritarian alternative to the present."[1] Within the German SDS, "there was a broad acceptance of council-democratic ideas," and Rudi Dutschke, central figure in the SDS "even drew up a rough sketch of a future Council Republic of West Berlin."

In France, Italy, and the United States, the story is similar. In the US, editorial projects, such as *Radical America*, which popularized the ideas of C. L. R. James, and *Root and Branch*, edited by Paul Mattick's son, Paul Mattick Jr., transmit council communist ideas to the New Left. In France, May '68 massively increases the prestige of several groups that had already placed the workers' council at the

1 Axel Weipert, *The Second Revolution: The Council Movement in Berlin 1919–20*, Historical Materialism Book Series, vol. 284 (Leiden: Brill, 2023), 10.

center of their theory, the Situationist International in particular. Dozens of council communist and pro-situ groups form during this period, initiating the debates about value described in the previous chapter.

This revival is, however, predicated on rather obscure currents traceable to the end of World War II who introduce novel elements into the theory of the workers' council and who begin to recognize historical developments in postwar capitalism which will require modification of the theory. Important to this story are dissidents from Trotskyism or official communism such as C. L. R. James and Raya Dunayevskaya in the United States, Cornelius Castoriadis and Claude Lefort in France, and the *Quaderni Rossi* group in Italy gathered around figures like Mario Tronti and Raniero Panzieri.[2]

These groups all brought something new to the concept of the council, however, something particular to this postwar era. This was the newfound thematic of "workers' inquiry" which, under various names, linked these groups. Workers' inquiry was the epistemological counterpart to workers' self-activity or self-organization—it was the representation of such self-activity in order to further it, to communicate possible tactics and methods to other workers. The seminal text here was *The American Worker*, written by the autoworker Phil Singer in collaboration with Grace Lee, and published in 1947 by the Johnson-Forest Tendency, a faction, led by C. L. R. James and Raya Dunayevskaya, that theorized its way out of Trotsky's Fourth International.[3] Like many others, notably Amadeo Bordiga, who re-entered Italian politics after the war thinking that a new era of proletarian offensive had begun, C. L. R. James saw in the end of the war the beginning of a new revolutionary sequence,

2 These are by no means the only figures involved in this revival—there are also the group around Marc Chirik, Union Communiste, and the groups around Serge Bricaner and Maximilien Rubel, which included many former POUMistas such as Grandizo Munis. This latter group was personally connected to Henk Canne Meijer of the GIK, and therefore established an important link between council communists before and after World War II. Another source for French interest in workers' inquiry is Rubel's reprinting of Marx's "Enquête ouvriére" in Maximilien Rubel, *Karl Marx. Essai de biographie intellectuelle* (Paris: M. Rivière, 1971).

3 Paul Romano and Ria Stone, *The American Worker* (Detroit: Bewick 1972 [1947]).

one that would emerge from the great postwar strike wave then underway. From Detroit, where James had settled after coming to the United States from England in 1938, James made connections with workers, particularly black workers and women, whose prospects had improved due to the wartime labor shortage, leading to a shakeup of the racial division of labor, as chronicled in the outstanding novel which James's friend, Chester Himes, wrote about a black worker in the wartime shipbuilding industry in Los Angeles, *If He Hollers Let Him Go.* Class collaborationist policies by unions and parties, modulating worker militancy in exchange for wage agreements and freedom from persecution, had driven resistance underground but also rendered the existing workers' organizations superficial. Once these policies ended with the war, unleashing a flood of workplace actions, James and his collaborators expected a revolutionary offensive similar to that of the 1917–23 period, this time undertaken against the collaborationist unions. Unlike the revolutions of this previous period, such a wave would take place independently of and even in opposition to the vanguard parties. This was because, for James, the work of the vanguard party had been completed. Whereas Karl Kautsky and Lenin had once been right that the proletariat needed the education of the party, the diploma had now been earned. Between 1938, when James had come to the US and visited Trotsky in Mexico, and 1947, when he charted his course away from Trotskyism, much had changed. Whereas in 1938, he was talking about workers' self-organization as a "school for planned economy" where "the proletariat will prepare itself for direct management of nationalized industry when the hour for that eventuality strikes," by 1947 he is writing that the hour has come:

> the workers no longer need to penetrate into any of the springs of capitalist economy. In some of the most important countries of the world the ruin and thievery of capitalist economy are open secrets to the workers. Workers' control of production by an [*sic*] derail plan becomes the sole means whereby it would be possible to rebuild the ruined nationalized economy.[4]

4 J. R. Johnson, *The Invading Socialist Society* (New York: Johnson-Forest Tendency, 1947).

For James, the workers no longer needed even the framework of the KAPD. This they already possessed, implicitly, though perhaps broken into fragments. The role of communists, then, is to catalyze not just self-organization but self-consciousness of already existing organization, bringing together and rendering explicit the tacit control over production which the proletariat already possesses. Whereas Trotsky-aligned activists in the Workers' Party or the Socialist Workers' Party might attempt to reorganize the workers in the Stalinist-aligned CIO or other unions, what James saw is that workers were appropriating these organizations to their own ends. It was thus the case that, paradoxically, after the collapse of the trade unions and the communist parties, "there is nothing more to organize … Organization as we have known it is at an end."[5] The workers were already organized—the trick was to make them conscious of that fact, to which end the Johnson-Forest Tendency produced texts like *The American Worker*, *Indignant Heart: A Black Worker's Journal*, and *A Woman's Place*, investigations of the role of workers, black workers, and women in advanced capitalist society that not only were for workers, black workers, and women, and about these groups, but also authored by them—self-authored, as it were, as expression of a revolutionary consciousness. The first text, for example, paired Phil Singer's observations and reflections about his time on the shop floor with Grace Lee's theoretical extrapolations. But the texts which the JFT produced were short on real inquiry and analysis, and they tended to generalize from a single case rather than conduct a systematic survey, as Asad Haider and Salar Mohandesi point out in their essay on the history of workers' inquiry.[6] This is because the object of these texts was less inquiry than the development of self-consciousness, less ground-clearing maneuver than rallying cry. If there was no more organizing to be done, then there was also no more inquiry to be done.

The expected working-class assault never arrived—the postwar strike wave was broken not just by anticommunism but by the dispiriting actions of communists themselves. It was not until the 1960s that

5 C. L. R. James, *Notes on Dialectics: Hegel, Marx, Lenin, Motive* (London: Allison & Busby, 1980), 117.

6 Asad Haider and Salar Mohandesi, "Workers' Inquiry: A Genealogy," *Viewpoint Magazine* 3, September 27, 2013, viewpointmag.com.

the kind of allies James and his group would have needed emerged, first within the Civil Rights Movement and eventually within Black Power, but by that time James had been expelled from the US, and though groups like the Sojourner Truth Organization and the League of Black Revolutionary Workers drew from his ideas, for the most part the spirit of the age unfolded differently.[7] Internationally, the most durable effect of the James group was its inspiration, elsewhere, of something that would be called, eventually, "workers' inquiry." In both France and Italy, *The American Worker* inspired imitators, but imitators who importantly recognized its weakness as inquiry and analysis and sought something other than testimonial. Exiled in France, James met with the members of Socialisme ou Barbarie, a group that also had emerged in a break with international Trotskyism, and which planned a much more ambitious workers' writing project—a workers' paper, *Tribune Ouvrière*, published out of the massive Renault factory at Billancourt (then the largest industrial site in France, the "fortress" of French capitalism), and which took much more seriously, to the point of tying itself in circles, the question of how such a publication should be written and produced, if workers' self-activity were to be not only the content but the form of such a project. Later, in Italy, the journal *Quaderni Rossi* would engage in a systematic rethinking of Leninism from the perspective of workers' self-activity, with Romano Alquati taking up and developing the theme of workers' inquiry in sophisticated new ways, where it would inspire a veritable tradition of such writing alive to this day.

The difference between the Americans and the French emerged from their entirely different attitudes to their fellow workers. For James, steeped in Hegel, the key term was "consciousness." For Socialisme ou Barbarie, who took some indications from French phenomenology and particularly Maurice Merleau-Ponty, the key term was "experience," as in the essay "Proletarian Experience," by Claude Lefort, which called for a process of workers' self-inquiry, an inquiry from the inside which took as starting point for its investigation of the labor-process in its objectivity the workers' own subjective

7 James returned to the US to teach in 1968, at the Federal City College in Washington, DC, but this does not seem to have strengthened his influence within the US New Left.

viewpoint. Unlike C. L. R. James, however, Claude Lefort did not imagine this process of inquiry as the extraction of an already-revolutionary subjectivity—rather the process of inquiry would itself be revolutionary, would itself catalyze revolutionary subjectivity. What the proletariat knew, it knew tacitly, not explicitly, and so such a process of inquiry would offer the working class "an opportunity to formalize, condense and confront types of knowledge usually implicit, more 'felt' than thought, and fragmentary."[8] This meant that Socialisme ou Barbarie would have to reflect directly not just on the content but on the form of such writing, which is to say not just the style of the writing itself but also the social and productive relations by which the writing was produced and distributed.

Tribune Ouvrière had emerged from the nucleus of a wildcat strike in a particular Billancourt department in 1947. Though members of Socialisme ou Barbarie would join the paper and attempt to remake it into an organ of workers' inquiry, this process was always prospective, and the original committee retained some control over the direction of the paper and continued to use it as an organ through which an active minority of workers might educate, propagandize, or lead the large mass of the class, no different from Lenin's party paper. In his reflection on his experience editing *Tribune Ouvrière*, Daniel Mothé lays out the problems facing a genuinely self-organized process of workers' writing: "How can the working class's ability to manage be developed? It's this question that the workers' paper must answer, not only in its content, but also in its very conception, and in its way of operating; which is to say it must itself be managed by workers."[9]

A true workers' paper would be the instrument whereby this capacity for self-management was developed. It would increasingly become not just in its content but in its form that "framework" for the organization of communism which the proletariat lacked. But then such a framework would not be a thing, an object, a document, or a computer program but rather the very process of proletarian self-consciousness developed in and through the paper. The paper

8 Claude Lefort, "Proletarian Experience (1952)," trans. Stephen Hastings-King, *Viewpoint Magazine* 3, September 26, 2013, viewpointmag.com.

9 Daniel Mothé, "The Problem of the Workers' Paper (1955)," *Viewpoint Magazine* 3, September 26, 2013, viewpointmag.com

would both grow the capacity for self-management and also be the realization of such capacity, without assuming, like James, that such a capacity already existed.

Within both *Tribune Ouvrière* and Socialisme ou Barbarie, members took a range of positions with regard to workers' inquiry—some adopted an "anarchist" position close to James and rejected any dialectic between militant editors and working-class writers; others simply wanted to use the paper as an instrument to agitate and organize the workers. In the context of the Algerian War and De Gaulle's coup in 1958, these factions effectively split apart, with Claude Lefort and others leaving to form Informations et Correspondances Ouvrières (ICO) along with many members of Socialisme ou Barbarie, including the council communist Henri Simon.[10] Though its documents typically speak abstractly about self-management rather than councils, ICO was a key vector in the revival of contemporary council communism. A network rather than an organization, in which all participants retained full autonomy, ICO swelled with new members after 1968, mainly students, but this student membership no longer allowed for organization in and as workers' inquiry. Many of the groups that succeeded ICO, such as Échanges et Mouvement, were explicitly council communist.

Whereas the James group thought self-organization already present if one simply knew where to look, and whereas Socialisme ou Barbarie imagined a dialectic between militants and self-organizing workers, ICO worried that intervention by militants would spoil the development of crucial working-class spontaneity. These positions might in some respect reflect their different historical moments—1947 vs. 1952, and 1952 vs. 1958. Like many communists, James expected a proletarian offensive to follow the end of the war, and at the time of writing the postwar strike wave might arguably have resembled the first moment of such a process. Later in the 1950s, however, during a more explicitly counter-revolutionary period, the terms changed from "consciousness" to "experience" and from "expression" to "inquiry." This was an extension of the theory of the communist left, a theory designed to produce communism in a

10 Henri Simon, "1958–1998: Communism in France: Socialisme ou Barbarie, ICO and Echanges" (1998), available at libcom.org, January 3, 2006.

revolutionary conjuncture, beyond its original context. The theory of the factory groups, for example, was never a theory of how to develop or measure the consciousness of the class, but to catalyze an already revolutionary consciousness. In the quietness of the 1950s, however, the absence of revolutionary prospects effectively meant that it was not clear what communists could or should do in non-revolutionary times. The answer that ICO comes up with is appealing: establish resonances, networks, and correspondences among the most revolutionary members of the class; pay attention, in order to discover the sources of class conflict, follow the new contours of class struggle, and anticipate the shape of coming self-activity.

A commitment to self-organization might, however, lead militants to conclude they must abolish themselves immediately, that a council communist party or organization is, in non-revolutionary times, a contradiction in terms. If the actions of dedicated intellectuals and militants could be counterproductive and not simply ineffective, then it was always possible nothing was better than something. The other alternative to liquidationism, the obverse extreme to which ICO had to respond, was an orientation to vanguard action, to leadership, and to acts of agitation and politicization, which the remaining members of Socialisme ou Barbarie still pursued. In 1960, when Guy Debord joined Socialisme ou Barbarie's political struggle group, Pouvoir Ouvrier, at a juncture when he and his partners in the Situationist International were rethinking their own orientation to vanguard action and incorporating a vision of communism and revolution which had the workers' council at its center, he encountered a group whose theory was in contradiction with its practice. Castoriadis had developed a model of class society applicable to both the USSR and France, actually existing socialism and actually existing capitalism, where social relations were those between director (or capitalist) and executant (or worker). But in the actual work of the group, Debord noticed, a division of labor still persisted, with most members orbiting one or another intellectual leader: "The division of society into directors and executants ... reappears under its corollary aspect of division between 'actors' and spectators."[11] Debord issued this

11 "Letter from Guy Debord to the Participants in the National Conference of *Pouvoir Ouvrier*" (May 5, 1961), trans. Bill Brown, available at notbored.org.

criticism of the group in a letter of resignation in which he made clear that he did not, by the same measure, support "Lefortism," and still imagined some interventive role for such groups while insisting, at the same time, that the division between leaders and followers need be abolished directly through such activity.

Nonetheless, the SI were the inheritors of these new left-communist ideas. From Socialisme ou Barbarie, they took a resolute commitment to working-class self-organization through the council form and opposition to state capitalism. From James, and from indications in the United States and elsewhere, they took a sense that insurrection was imminent, self-organization everywhere and unacknowledged, and the proletariat already intuitively aware of its renewed mission. Once freed from the burden of developing consciousness or organizing workers directly, the SI could become a theoretical and interventive organ without followers, oriented toward experiment, elaboration, direct action, and speculation. The SI conceived of itself as a catalytic instrument in a larger process of mass self-organization—a catalyst rather than mechanism, because the role of the group was to abolish itself in the process of insurrection, after which direct communist self-organization would emerge, obviating the need for a leading party. This is very close to the original vision of Appel, both in his Hempel speech and in the *Grundprinzipien*. Though the SI did not imagine themselves possessor of a framework precisely, they did embrace a notion of revolution that aimed toward a fusion of anarchism and Marxism, centered on the council, here instrument of a "generalized self-management" that would exceed the bounds of the workplace proper.

The group's optimism served it well and made it uniquely sensitive to signs of disorder, to proletarian insurgency in locales both likely and unlikely, allowing them effectively to anticipate in both theory and practice the coming global '68. Pivoting away from intervention in the sphere of culture and art directly, as a result not only of their encounter with groups like S. ou B. but the failure of such experiments in the face of a mature capitalism, they quickly think themselves to the limits of communist theory as it existed. As early as 1962, in their essay "The Bad Days Will End," which references both Correspondence and Socialisme ou Barbarie, they read from the tea leaves of a comparatively minor smattering of worker revolts what will more or less become the structuring logic of revolt in the coming era, featuring attacks not only against the machinery of production, but also that of consumption, transportation, communication, and information—in other words, the nerve-plexus of advanced industrial capitalism.[12] Focusing strictly on actions by workers and excluding the actions of "youth" and "adolescents" they elsewhere champion, they note that the workers are no longer struggling explicitly against the conditions of work but also attacking the "machines of consumption."

Like Appel, they describe an old workers' movement and a new one. While the essay begins by describing European society as a "televised Elsinore castle whose political mists are dissipated as soon as workers councils come into existence and for as long as they reign," the forms of worker self-organization the essay details are only sometimes directed against their conditions of work.[13] In celebrating the destruction of the cars of their fellow workers by miners, the sabotage of newspaper facilities during a general strike, and the riot of factory workers in Naples, they detail a shift away from production as the exclusive site of struggle and a newly general antagonism directed likewise at consumption and distribution. Because it calls into question the pseudo-satisfactions of consumer society, such an antagonism also sings the end of a "militant" politics defined by discipline and duty, and inaugurates a newly festive politics whose "revolutionary associations of a new type will … break with the old world by permitting and demanding of its members an authentic and creative participation." Here we see something largely new in communist revolutionary theory, which the SI derive from the artistic avant-garde: the idea that revolutionary groups should exemplify in their conduct the new forms of life which revolution will bring—if revolution involves among other things creative liberation, then revolutionaries both before and during the revolution will need to be creatively liberated. As a result:

---

12 Situationist International, "The Bad Days Will End," in *Situationist International Anthology* (Berkeley, CA: Bureau of Public Secrets, 2006), 107–14.

13 Ibid., 107.

> The groups that recognize the fundamental (not merely circumstantial) failure of the old politics must also recognize that they can claim to be an *ongoing avant-garde* only if they themselves exemplify a new style of life, a new passion. There is nothing utopian about this lifestyle criterion: it was constantly evident during the emergence and rise of the classical workers movement. We believe that in the coming period this will not only hold true to the extent it did in the nineteenth century, but will go much further. Otherwise the militants of these groups would only constitute dull propaganda societies, proclaiming quite correct and basic ideas but with virtually no one listening. The spectacular unilateral transmission of a revolutionary teaching—whether within an organization or in its action directed toward the outside—has lost all chance of proving effective in the society of the spectacle, which simultaneously organizes a completely different spectacle and infects every spectacle with an element of nausea. Such specialized propaganda thus has little chance of leading to timely and fruitful intervention during situations when the masses are compelled to wage real struggles.[14]

With this, the SI add something new to the discourse of left communism and council communism, something that finds affinity in the anarchist communism of Kropotkin and Malatesta, which had often emphasized the continuity of anarchist principles in capitalism and after it, thus blurring the line between the organization of anarchists in capitalism and the organization of anarchism or socialism as such. While Appel and the KAPD imagined a party which was a "nucleus" in which each individual could act autonomously according to right principle and provide the framework for the self-organization of communism, they did not necessarily insist that the ethics of such groups anticipate communism through a new style of life. There was no "lifestyle criterion" for the KAPD, even if the armed bands practiced a crude egalitarianism. For Debord, however, though he subscribed to Appel's notion of the party as catalytic converter, the framework which the KAPD thought need be embodied in doctrine was more importantly for the SI demonstrated by the actions and gestures of proletarians themselves. Theory was immanent in proletarian practice and communicated directly by it, and therefore

14 Ibid., 112.

the blueprint for communism was already legible in the sabotages, refusals, and expropriations of a rebellious proletarian youth, putting to queer uses the abundance of postwar society. This meant that however much they centered workers or workers' councils in their vision they saw the entire society and not just the workplace as a laboratory for the development of communism. To the projects of inquiry of Socialisme ou Barbarie they added an expanded field, beyond the factories, looking to new forms of organization and new tactics by proletarians—and not just workers—across the world, with special attention to the forms of action of young proletarians, often denoted as strictly criminal and frequently racialized. For the SI, whose connections to the working class were tenuous, such an inquiry could be conducted through an examination of what proletarians do. There was no need for Lefortian phenomenology, only reporting. What proletarians thought could be seen in their actions, and the SI were among the first to descry in these actions what will eventually be called, by Mario Tronti and others, a "strategy of refusal" or "refusal of labor," an antagonism toward work and a desire for immediate, creative fulfillment that might find expression in vandalism, sabotage, and riot.[15] In particular, it could be seen in the festive character that proletarian struggle took on, even and perhaps especially when violent.

As noted, this theory more or less anticipates many aspects of the global '68 and in particular May '68 in France. A volatile group with few members, the SI played a minor, instigating role in the actual events of May—largely through their influence on the March 22 Movement in Strasbourg and their publication of *On the Poverty of Student Life*—but a major role in the ideological crystallizations by which the event was understood, contributing deeply to the language, theory, and visual culture of the moment and the movement. People read the slogans of the SI on the walls and adopted their attitudes at a gestural level without, perhaps, having read any of the relevant texts. As a result, in the aftermath of May, the theoretical luster of council communism increased massively, such that one could now speak of an "ultraleft" milieu, vaguely influenced by the SI and Socialisme ou Barbarie but seeking out a theory adequate to the moment. In some

15 Mario Tronti, *Workers and Capital* (New York: Verso, 2019), 241–62.

sense "council communism" is a retroactive reconstruction of this moment of broad ultraleft revival—1918 as seen by 1968.

This is, of course, in keeping with the way that council communists like Appel and Mattick conceived of theory—the theory of the council was, we remember, a product of history, a clarification of something the revolutionary proletariat had already begun to work out for itself, at least intuitively. A return of the theory of the council would be meaninglessness unless accompanied by conciliar practice, whatever that meant. This was something history provided. Nikita Khrushchev's secret speech of 1956, which opened the door to criticism of Stalin within official communism, was followed, later that year, by the Hungarian Revolution of 1956 in which workers' councils called for general strikes and assumed power over the economy before being crushed by the Soviet Army. The Cultural Revolution—about which very little real information but many distortions could be found—also seemed to indicate a period of revolutionary self-activity against Communist Party bureaucratization with newly formed committees, councils, militias, and communes.

At first, May '68 seemed like the echo of this sequence on the other side of the wall. After the factory occupations spread in mid-May, the Situationist International installed itself in the occupied Sorbonne, formed the Council for the Maintenance of the Occupations, and called for the formation of workers' councils which could throw off the yoke of the unions, arm the workers, and initiate the tasks of revolution. But this meta-council, like the worker and student action committees at the occupied Censier campus of the Sorbonne, where every faction of the ultraleft was represented, served only to underscore the absence of real councils in the occupied factories. Once the unions concluded that the factory occupations could not be stopped, they easily made themselves representatives of the movement, a fact that, in hindsight, could be attributed only to the inability or unwillingness of the workers to form rank-and-file organizations in order to oppose them, as had happened in Germany in 1918. This hesitancy on the part of the class must be attributed in part to the origin of the uprising in the university, but also more broadly to a "critique of separation" which aimed, sometimes in the most voluntaristic manner possible, to overcome all the divisions that prohibited the proletariat from uniting. This included the division of labor, represented chiefly by the division between the university (mental labor) and the factories (manual labor), but also the divisions between immigrant and French labor, and between the French Communist Party and the international communist movement. University students were opposed to regimes of testing that introduced arbitrary divisions among them, and this was something with which young workers, themselves divided by arbitrary job classifications, could identify. Refusal of labor was above all a refusal of these identifications, whether student or worker. One reason why workers didn't self-organize in the factories according to their job specification, then, is that the very movement was opposed to such specification. The most activated proletarians gathered together outside of the workplace, in the worker-student action committees at occupied Censier, for example.

Even though the anti-Bolshevist poetry of the SI set the tone of the events, many participants responded to the critique of separation by becoming militants—that is, dedicating themselves, as intellectuals, to serving the people or leading them, as many variants of Maoism and Marxism-Leninism then insisted they must. Militantism was the métier of the Maoist student groups, but it affected the ultraleft as well, as we learn from Fredy Perlman and Roger Gregoire's excellent firsthand account and analysis of the Censier occupation.[16] After the factory occupations were stalled by the unions, there was broad awareness of a need to unite across the campuses and the workplaces and hence the famous action committees were formed. At Censier, Perlman participated in the Citroën Action Committee, and he narrates a paradigmatic march out of Censier and to the gates of the occupied Citroën factory where the assorted workers and students were met by union representatives, who kept them from entering the factory and mediated their communication with the workers. On the first day that this march arrived, it collaborated with the union to get striking foreign workers—some of the participants in the action committees were also immigrants, who spoke the same languages as these workers—to enter the strike. But that night, reflecting on

16 Fredy Perlman and Roger Gregoire, *Worker-Student Action Committees, France May '68* (Detroit: Black & Red, 1969). The vectors of influence went the other way as well, as can be seen in Mao-spontex tendency—Maoist and spontaneist—and specifically the Gauche Prolétarienne.

events, they decided not to work with the union any longer and to return to the gates, issuing a call for the workers to unite in a general assembly which could directly speak for and organize the workers against the unions:

> The occupied factories have to be opened up to all comrades, workers as well as students, in order to enable them to make decisions together.
>
> Workers and students have the same objectives. Despite the government, the universities are already open to all.
>
> If the loudspeakers decide instead of you, if the loudspeakers broadcast the decisions "we" have made, then the men behind the loudspeakers are not working with you; they're manipulating you.[17]

These calls were, of course, drowned out by the union and hence the action committee sought the workers at their homes, outside of the workplace, indicating its weakness but also its new areas of power.

Here we have an archetypal encounter, the very grammar of '68 and much else besides. In the first place, the self-organizing workers, a furnace of negativity, which can strike the workplace but not organize it. Then the unions, substituting themselves for the workers, representing them to the employers, the state, and the public, but doing so without really being contested at all by the workers. Next, the activist mob—intellectuals, students, unemployed workers, striking workers from other workplaces—which did display antagonism to the unions, but from the other side of the factory gates. Its options were to replace the union, offering its own leadership, as the Maoist and Marxist-Leninist groups did; to serve as an auxiliary, encouraging self-organization, as the Citroën Action Committee did; or perhaps to do nothing whatsoever, like the members of ICO, who met in a separate room in Censier and did not participate in the action committees.

There was a fourth option, which was to stop being a Citroën Action Committee and instead orient toward projects which were within the grasp of the group's members and, more importantly, met their needs. This would require giving up militantism altogether

17 Ibid., 26

but also, importantly, treating the "self" of self-organization with exceeding care. Who was it exactly that organized in the universities, in the factories? In hindsight, Perlman and Gregoire write, the action committees had misunderstood the radicality of the student occupations and the movement altogether: "The 'students' did not 'take over' the universities. At the Sorbonne, Censier, Nanterre and elsewhere, the university was proclaimed social property, the universities became ex-universities. The buildings were opened to the entire society—to students, teachers, workers—to anyone who wanted to come."[18] These "general assemblies" then "were not instances of self-organization by students over 'their own' affairs" but simply "instances of self-organization by the people inside of a specific building, whatever their specializations." The implications of this misrecognition are profound, since it means that, in fact, as "social property" the Citroën plant belongs no more to those inside the gates than outside. Armed with this recognition, Perlman and Gregoire wonder what would have happened if the action committee had responded to union perfidy by listening to the suggestion of some of its members and occupying the national radio broadcasting station, speaking directly to the workers through the airwaves. What held participants back was the logic of militantism which said that only the radio workers themselves could strike the towers. To whom should such a radio tower belong? To the radio tower workers? Or to all revolutionary communists?

Perlman and Gregoire were moved to this critique through a careful reading of Guy Debord and the Situationist International, whom they came into contact with during the Censier occupation. Perlman returned to Michigan after '68, where he would found Black & Red, the English-language publishers of Debord, the SI, and a good portion of the ultraleft content mentioned here. He also published *Eclipse and Re-emergence of the Communist Movement*, by Gilles Dauvé and François Martin, already discussed in the last chapter, which provides an account of the events of May that argues very similarly to Perlman and Gregoire about the limits of self-organization that had been reached at Censier, developing from there a fuller account of the implication of these limits for the

18 Ibid., 71.

development of communism.[19] As Dauvé tells us in a more recent piece of writing, participants at Censier held ideas about workers' democracy as a path toward liberation that proved unserviceable in the unfolding of May:

> Because we believed in worker councils as a means to achieve self-management of everyday life, we stood for worker democracy, providing it was authentic (not manipulated by bureaucrats or politicians), and for self-management, providing it was generalised. This was indeed the prevailing mood in the Censier committees. But as it unfolded before our eyes, the reality of the strike went against this belief.
>
> Initially, in many factories, without any formal decision-making meeting, a radical minority had imposed the work stoppage upon the majority. Later, as the strike went on, union officials had used debates and majority votes to wear out the movement. Democratic criteria such as proper expression of collective will, discussion prior to action, and majority control over decisions proved useless to understand the launching of the strike, let alone contribute to it. When faced with a minority act, no formal criterion would have been enough to determine if the minority was acting as a constraint upon the majority, or initiating an action supported by the general will. The same gesture (welding the factory doors, for example) took on a different meaning according to the circumstances.
>
> When most of us (myself included, in my study of the failed Russian revolution) upheld worker democracy, it was not for the sake of renovating parliamentarianism, but because self-managing one's struggle was a necessary step on the way to self-managing production. Therefore, reexamining democracy led us to question the priority usually given to the whole issue of management.[20]

As discussed earlier, Dauvé and Martin developed this critique of democracy based on their own experience of struggle not from the SI but from the postwar writing of Amadeo Bordiga, who had made criticism of liberal-democratic ideas within the socialist movement

19 Jean Barrot (Gilles Dauvé) and François Martin, *Eclipse and Re-emergence of the Communist Movement*, 1st ed. (Detroit: Black & Red, 1974).

20 Gilles Dauvé, *From Crisis to Communisation* (Oakland, CA: PM Press, 2019).

a central part of his notion of Marxist orthodoxy. An engineer by training, Bordiga saw the party as a technical device, a functional means to an objective end, and something of a black box. What mattered was that it worked, that it produced revolution and communism, not how it did so. The function of the party was to produce communism, to organize communism directly, beginning from some revolutionary moment. What was paramount, then, for the party was its objective, something which could be defined concretely as a series of tasks, as aspects of capitalism or class society to be abolished, and as new relations to be established. This was the content of communism and also the function of the party.

Bordiga was famously indifferent to means—his treatment of communism as an end, as content, could become a kind of Platonism, an endorsement of communism as enlightened technocracy, and also a kind of by-any-means-sufficient opportunism. But if freedom is the essence of communism, as Marx believed, then one cannot be indifferent to form. And as Debord acknowledges, people only fight for something that makes their lives better. Whether it embodies it or affects it, a theory of communism can't avoid the question of proletarian motives or desire, so clearly raised by '68. Dauvé's essay "Sur l'idéologie ultragauche" borrowed from Bordiga to criticize the deficiencies within the ultraleft, particularly council communism, while still retaining its emphasis on working-class self-organization, desires, and motives.[21] The text was addressed to a gathering which ICO had called for the summer of 1969, and which council communists in France and elsewhere would attend. Through a curious logic of exemplification, the fact that ICO had convoked the meeting and therefore called into question what all these groups shared allowed Dauvé to make them an example of an entire contemporary current and historical tradition.

From Bordiga, Dauvé derives the salient idea that communism is not a form of management (or distribution), and thus proletarian self-management by workers' councils is insufficient as a definition of communism. Communism must be the destruction of the law of

21 Gilles Dauvé, "Sur l'ideologie ultra-gauche," in François Danel, ed., *Rupture dans la théorie de la révolution: Textes 1965–75* (Geneva: Entremonde, 2018), 205–15.

value—something that is not a matter of management or form alone but of the very material structure of capitalism. A group which commits itself to stating facts such as these, derived from theory, need not fear the role it will play with regard to proletarian self-organization, as ICO did at Censier, when its fear of leading drove it to what Debord calls a "choice of nonexistence." Like Perlman and Gregoire, Dauvé sees the ultraleft as the guilty, inverted image of the militant—both the fear of the party and the desire for it betray a lack of faith in the capacities of proletarians and reinscribe the division between revolutionary proletarians and revolutionary communists, which must be overcome. This is the necessary result of a theory of communism which defines communism as a form of organization rather than an objective to be realized, a series of tasks. If communism is not a matter of formal organization but of objectives and aims in movement, then ICO's anxiety of influence, its worry that it would spoil proletarian self-activity by constituting itself as a coherent group with a position, was misplaced. For Dauvé, the problems of '68 were not so much organizational as historical—the separation of communist intellectuals, the movement of communists, from the workers' movement, which would have to be basis for a communist movement, derives ultimately from the division of labor in capitalist society, and chiefly the division between mental and manual labor. In insurrection and revolution, these divisions are overcome through the process of making revolution—intellectuals and workers unite not as leaders and led but as participants in a process both practical and theoretical all at once. This is what had begun to happen at Censier, and the self-isolation of ICO, worried that they might pollute a pure proletarian essence, had deeply missed the point.

"Ultraleft" is a term that Dauvé utilizes in order to speak at once about a few groups, a broad milieu, and a historical tradition—previously the term had been largely a pejorative one used by Leninists in order to speak of an infantile "left deviation." In naming these groups ultraleft, Dauvé emphasizes how they are predicated negatively on the central principles of the social-democratic and Bolshevist left, on opposition to a left orthodoxy whose position they must invert. Dauvé sees a red thread linking the AAUD-E (which split from the KAPD in 1920 and insisted the factory groups themselves were sufficient), the Dutch-German GIK, and ICO, all of whom refuse the party as a figure of pedagogical or pastoral leadership. Here, drawing from Bordiga, he distinguishes between, on the one hand, the formal party, and on the other, what he calls the historical party, which may not even be recognizable as a party at all. Opposition to groups establishing themselves as the centralizing, decision-making vanguard of the revolution is one thing, but a revolution is not simply the absence of vanguard—it is a historical process which must be accomplished by proletarians themselves, who must organize themselves in order to abolish capitalism. Whatever form this takes, we know it will take a form, and this is what we might call the historical party, which may not even recognize itself as a party. The party is not simply a form, an organization, but also a content, a function—that is to say, the overcoming of capitalism and the production of communism. Dauvé writes:

> For Marx the party is nothing but the spontaneous organization (that's to say totally determined by social development) of the revolutionary movement produced by capitalism. The party grows spontaneously from the historical ground of modern society. The wish to create the party and the fear of creating it are equally illusory.[22]

For Dauvé, following this particular reading of the Marxian party as function rather than form, the party must take as its object the overcoming of the division of labor, which is the root of divisions within the working class and also between the working class and the bourgeoisie. It cannot be simply an organization of the movement of communists—that is to say, of intellectuals—as most parties are, and as groups like ICO recognized, but neither can it be simply the working class itself, those working-class organizations which the class uses to improve its position within capitalism. Militantism attempts to forcibly seal the gap between the workers' movement and the communist movement, whereas non-intervention imagines it can somehow abnegate the entire intellectual layer, leaving the working class suddenly free to organize itself without the meddling of well-meaning intellectuals. Neither are likely to overcome the sources of these divisions, which lie in everyday life, in the built environment, and within the division of labor more broadly.

22 Ibid., 209. Translation mine.

Organizing as labor does not overcome the division of labor; only organizing against labor does, and that is something that can happen only during conjunctures in which mass refusal of labor is possible. The gap is not a hole in organization, then, but a hole in history.

But what is left after Dauvé's intervention, which dissolves rather than resolves the famous Leninist question: What to do? Communism may not be a system of management or organization alone, but conceiving of it this way allows for communists to present communism as a framework—a plan, a structure—and to be able to point to concrete organizational forms, like the councils, that might be put in place as intermediate steps. It is one thing to say that the councils alone are insufficient, but does this mean they are unnecessary? And what do we mean by council, precisely? What was the historical and what the formal party in the Ruhr, in Barcelona? In each case, we see structures of what we might call proletarian autonomy, structures whose character is ambiguously revolutionary. In each instance, a section of the class separates itself from the class and its counter-class and insists on its autonomy without committing itself definitely to the abolition of the counter-class and therefore itself. Here form is radical, for it forces something radical, a breakdown in the reproduction of capitalism. But it is not necessarily revolutionary in content: unless it commits to abolition of capital, autonomy from capitalism will always be autonomy within capitalism, a contradiction in terms. In the Commune, as we know, the communards hesitated to destroy the Versaillese, to nationalize the banks, and to make communism. In the Ruhr, partisans of the council fought to avoid being disarmed but not to make communism. In May, the working class rose up to refuse work, to insist on its autonomy, but it could not or would not attempt to formalize that autonomy, leaving settlement to the arbiters of labor power. No armed guards were formed to vouchsafe proletarian autonomy. This was both a continuation of the logic of the prior sequence and its completion. Something had been glimpsed by the proletariat and could not thereafter be unseen. Autonomy could no longer be a stepping-stone on the way to communism, as capitalism had already shown itself capable of rendering this autonomy within capitalism a source of heteronomy. Autonomy thereafter could be only negative—appearing as refusal, secession, and expropriation that also refuses any common program or organizational unity.

Communist revolution as communization would be a process of fission—one-sided communist measures that break apart the enterprises and structures of everyday life, provoking further measures, until something like a critical mass is achieved. And yet, in order to reproduce themselves, to persist, new forms will need to emerge in the wake of such a process. Are we sure they will not be councils of a sort, if by councils we mean "*self-reflexive responsivity to natural and social conditions in the process of their collective transformation by individuals*"?[23]

For Bordiga, there is nothing new in capitalism or its theory. The theory of communism has been invariant since 1848. The errors of communist theory and practice described above derive from doctrine, and the improper maintenance of Marxist theory by revisionists. But it is one thing to say that the workers' movement put one foot forward, then failed to put the next foot forward; it is another thing to say that it should have leapt on the first foot, or skipped. Were the workers' councils simply insufficient, as might have been recognized by council communists themselves, or were they an active impediment, as Bordiga thought? This is where the theory of the historical party would need a historical theory and a theory of crisis, which Bordiga himself lacked. The main point of the council communists is that the councils were revolutionary because the workers had chosen them, spontaneously, as the engine with which to overturn capitalism. Even if they were themselves impediment, one would still need to start there, with the revolutionary example. What is different about 1968 is that the working class refused not just work but also the formation of councils, except in a few instances. Self-organization could not proceed through the workers' councils, which seemed like they would obviously be controlled by the unions. There was no way to imagine a better life that way. Why? What had changed? The answer would need to be sought in the changing nature of the production process and everyday life, structures of the division of labor which made the councils seem impossible.

This critique of council communism might seem in retrospect to have been arrived at rather directly by participants in the events

23 A New Institute for Social Research, "Theses on the Council Concept," 2019, isr.press.

of May in France, the US 1960s, or the Italian 1970s. But in fact things looked rather different to many in the 1970s within the broad "ultraleft," who saw in the shape of the events in France and later events—in Portugal, Chile, Poland, Iran—not the death rites of the council form but its renascence. Councils or attempts to form them appeared in each of these cases, a clustering that, by comparison with other decades, seems remarkable. Portugal was particularly singled out as a conciliar revolution. Following just six years upon the French May, and with a proximity that enabled many militants to travel there from France (or England, or Italy, or elsewhere) to participate in events, Portugal seemed to figures as diverse as Louis Althusser and Debord to offer a redux of May, one that might succeed or fail but would nonetheless feature the same elements along with some crucial new ones.

The SI had collapsed after May '68, though in truth it had never really much existed as an actual organization beyond Debord's expulsive whims. Debord eventually retired from direct political intervention, devoting himself to reflecting on the world and his own experiences. But for a moment he vacillated, contemplating a return to active politics. No political scene was more tempting to him than Portugal, the events of which he followed closely and hoped to influence from afar. Debord's correspondence was vast—he maintained contact even with people who had been expelled from his organization, and during this period corresponded with and sent specific instructions to his contacts in Portugal and those on their way there, indicating what they might do to hasten the unfolding of the social revolution.[24] His analysis drew directly from May and from what the SI had done there, and he was disappointed that his contacts in Portugal, who organized and propagandized largely by drawing from SI texts and from Debord's letters to them, had not even attempted to do in Portugal what he and his associated had done with the Council for the Maintenance of the Occupations. Debord's contact in Lisbon, Afonso Monteiro, a Portuguese exile who had translated *Society of the Spectacle*, set up a Conselho para

24 Ricardo Noronha, "Letters from 'Glaucos': The Correspondence of Guy Debord during the Portuguese Revolution," *Historical Materialism: Research in Critical Marxist Theory* 28, no. 4 (2020): 176–201.

o Desenvolvimento da Revolução Social and began agitating for the workers' committees and occupied factories that had formed to declare their autonomy from the Portuguese Communist Party (PCP) and its front groups and offshoots. But he lacked the depth of contacts that Debord and his network had in Paris.

Debord's main complaint was that Monteiro had not let the world know what was happening in Portugal, had not used the moment to popularize the autonomy of the workers' councils and other neighborhood assemblies that had formed, and to warn against the state-capitalist project of alliance formed between the PCP and the right wing of the Movement of the Armed Forces (MFA), who had hoped to engage in purges of corporatist appointees from the fascist regime within industrial management and thereby put the country on a more solid, technocratic, and state-capitalist path to industrialization, without allowing an opening for the workers' movement. The mainstream of the MFA was putatively socialist but, for the most part, really just populist. Decolonization and antifascism were, for them, screens behind which they could complete the industrial transition that the agrarian, clerical, and traditionalist fascism of Salazar could not. Debord and his associates in Paris were instead to develop an account of the revolution on their own, publishing *La guerre sociale au Portugal*, by Jaime Semprun, based on correspondence and research but little direct experience.[25]

Accounts closer to the grain of events will nonetheless confirm Debord's sense of the events in Portugal as revealing something about the logic of May '68.[26] The Portuguese Revolution recapitulates the lessons of the Commune and the workers' councils of 1917–23, and tests them against the emerging conditions of the postwar order, disclosing what still remains true and what has changed. Because Portugal was comparatively underdeveloped economically, and its

---

25 Jaime Semprun, *La guerre sociale au Portugal* (Paris: Editions Champs Libres, 1975).

26 Phil Mailer, *Portugal, the Impossible Revolution?*, Black Rose Books, F32 (London: Solidarity, 1977); Charles Reeve, *The Development of Workers' Self-Organization*, vol. 6, Root & Branch Pamphlet (Root & Branch, 1976). See also Loren Goldner, *Ubu Saved from Drowning: Worker Insurgency and Statist Containment in Portugal and Spain, 1974–1977*, Marx/Third Millennium Series (Cambridge, MA: Queequeg Publications, 2000).

political system a holdover from interwar fascism, the events of the Portuguese Revolution repeat many of the lessons of Germany and Spain. But because the events in Portugal are precipitated by the worldwide process of decolonization, by the end of the Bretton Woods monetary system, the 1973 oil shock, and the new international division of labor in which Portuguese manufacturing became attractive to overseas firms, many elements are quite new, and we can see in the surfeit of workers' committees, neighborhood committees, popular assemblies, and other base formations, the shape of revolution in the decades that follow, and the new problems this will pose. In Portugal, as with the other late conciliar revolutions—in Chile, Poland, or Iran—councils or something like them form very broadly, throughout a part of the industrial base. But in none of them do the councils project or move toward a break with capitalist reproduction—on the contrary, inasmuch as self-management or autonomy is projected by these councils it is an autonomy that requires, paradoxically, the support of the state. The radicality of autonomy increasingly becomes a radicality of form that accepts and even effects a reformist content. Nonetheless, we cannot blame communists for seeing in these councils a communist potential, for that is what the era could recall of the 1917–23 sequence.

In Portugal the problem of the army and the arming of the workers looms very large—reminding us of Marx's first lesson of the revolution—destruction of the standing army. As in Germany, the army had been largely neutralized as a peacekeeping force, leaving the ruling class without recourse to organized violence against the workers. But only in Germany did the workers really arm themselves, which points to the subtle weakness of the Portuguese case and the new disposition of the working class. Unlike the vast soldiers' mutiny that ended World War I, the Movement of the Armed Forces that precipitated the Portuguese Revolution in 1974 was an officers' revolt, mounted against the losing war effort in the African colonies of Angola, Mozambique, and Guinea-Bissau, where Portugal's sons were being sent to die fighting a guerrilla resistance many recognized as morally just. The MFA, then, must be understood as having forestalled a collapse of the army in desertion and mutiny like Germany—a collapse which would have meant a movement among the rank and file rather than the officers, who were largely of middle-class background. Rank-and-file struggle organizations in the barracks took longer to develop and never escaped the shadow of the MFA. Nonetheless, the MFA severely diminished the police power of the Portuguese state with regard to workers' self-activity. There was no consistent enforcement of employers' and landlords' ownership rights, which had the effect of making the social explosion in Portugal quite radical—so radical, in fact, that the unfinished business in the army could be mistakenly overlooked. The non-collapse of the army backstopped the collapse of the state and kept any political unit from asserting control—such that there was a great flourishing of radical political tendencies, including ultraleft ones. Newspapers and radios carried programs that were ultraleft in orientation, right next to Stalinist or Marxist-Leninist programs. In Portugal to an extent greater perhaps than anywhere in the world, all the positions discussed here were debated outright by a mass movement whose extent relative to the Portuguese population was quite significant, at a level equally as high as the mobilizations discussed earlier.

This happened alongside a mass strike whose extent and ferocity was impressive, at least given the relatively underdeveloped nature of Portuguese capitalism. The Portuguese Revolution was, first and foremost, an antifascist revolution against the post-Salazar state, and so its first acts were typically *saneamentos* (purges) of managers, administrators, and owners connected to Salazar appointees or the political police. In this it recapitulates the lessons of antifascism visible first during the Kapp Putsch and underlined even more severely by the Spanish Civil War. The reactive mass strike fails where it only rises to the defense of the republic. Even though the MFA and its allies in the Portuguese Communist Party tried to convince workers not to strike and not to ask for wage increases, workers self-organized exactly as the previous sequence would lead us to expect, forming workplace committees which, in several cases, became the de facto managers of their workplaces, because the managers and owners had fled. This was no small fraction of the Portuguese economy—by 1975, 380 workplaces were under self-management, and there were thousands of workplace committees. In the south, agricultural workers had occupied over 300 different tracts, in many cases land left fallow by the owners of large latifundia; by September it was estimated that over 10,000 workers had occupied close to 400,000 hectares. One must add to this hundreds of neighborhood committees, housing occupations, popular assemblies, and rank-and-file soldiers' organizations, which, borrowing from the new tactical repertoire of the global '68, attempted to fuse these organizations together outside of the control of the parties and the MFA. But because these groups thought they might count on the support of left factions within the MFA, no serious attempt to arm the councils was made.

In place of a real Red Army, a non-army like the one that had formed in the Ruhr, there were instead maverick brigades under the control of politicized officers. Here in particular the example of the COPCON, the security force of the MFA, under the command of General Otelo Carvalho, looms particularly large. COPCON was effectively the only police force in Portugal that could be called upon to resolve workplace disputes. They had earned a reputation for siding with the actions of autonomous workers—called to the premises of *La Republica*, the main morning newspaper, whose workers had formed a committee and ejected the socialist-aligned editorial board, they decided not to intervene, effectively siding with the workers—at the same time as they violently enforced the prerogatives of capital elsewhere. Before the revolution, the Portuguese left consisted of various vanguard groups, many engaged in underground work and armed struggle. But the emergence of the mass strike, the workers' committees, and the neighborhood assemblies led many participants of these groups to move toward an embrace of the workers' council and a support of the autonomous workers' movement. LUAR, for example, had been an armed-struggle group which had split from the PCP, formed by the charismatic Hermínio da Palma Inácio to oppose the Salazar regime and its colonial efforts—they hijacked planes to distribute leaflets over Lisbon, robbed banks to fund their efforts, raided armories to arm themselves, and even attempted to occupy the small town of Covilhã. After the fall of the regime, however, its members adopted positions that ran "from Luxemburgist to council communism" and became a "service group" that could be called upon by the movement to occupy houses. Luxemburgist or Spartacist in orientation also was the PRP-BR, formed by the underground Revolutionary Brigades that had also split from the PCP, inspired by Che Guevara's program for popular armed struggle. After the revolution, they also devoted themselves to the autonomous councils and assemblies, forming the People's Revolutionary Party. At the climax of the revolutionary wave, where a definitively capitalist Group of Nine had proposed a path to the restoration of class rule, the PRP and COPCON made an alternate proposal to empower workers' councils. Because the workers' commission and committees were largely unorganized and had been recuperated by agents of the PCP and various Maoist militants, they attempted to start a different organizational structure, with real councils, related through a definitive delegative structure. But this effort was too late, and the penetration of these revolutionary councils was not very deep.

In hindsight, this alliance with COPCON seems mistaken and perhaps betrays the shallowness of the PRP's support for the councils. While some units of the COPCON may have been genuinely committed to the revolution and even to the autonomy of the assemblies, the very structure of the army and the officers' movement within it ran counter to the grain of true conciliar power, which if we will remember had been introduced in Germany by mutiny. The rank-and-file groups were not a source of practical or political power, which still lay in the hands of individual officers whose loyalty or alliance had to be secured ideologically. There was no real conciliar power in the army, and in fact most of the MFA and the soldiers accepted that such a thing was a contradiction in terms. And yet, naively many suspected they might count on the COPCON to backstop the councils. There were limited attempts to arm the workers themselves, and the workers who were armed provided no resistance when the day came that the hierarchy within the army shuffled COPCON off and reorganized itself around the right wing of the movement. There could be no resistance, since commitment to the revolution, in the terms of the MFA, meant commitment to the very apparatus of the counter-revolution. The surprising fragility of the revolution here is one of the many ways in which it echoes the anticlimax of '68 and also other moments, such as the resistance to Augusto Pinochet's 1973 coup, which had been long anticipated by the communist left in Chile who had formed workers' councils preventatively and occupied much of the industrial base near the Chilean capital but in the end fired hardly a shot in defense of Salvador Allende. Their cached arms remained buried.

The Portuguese Revolution confirmed the suppositions of soixante-huitard council communists that a new era of councils arrived, and yet it provided a situation in which those councils were by their nature not only inadequate to the task at hand but forced to work at cross-purposes and to undermine the construction of conciliar power. Even if they had armed themselves and forestalled the counter-revolution of the Movement of the Nine, they would have had to confront the fact that the councils which had fallen under self-management were dependent upon the state as it existed and capitalism. In Portugal a unique dynamic came into play which would in fact come to characterize the coming era as such and make workers' self-management incompatible with the project of emancipation. Significant here was the fact that conciliar power did not emerge in one fell swoop, and because there was limited union penetration, not all workplaces had councils. But the Portuguese industry in the south was both concentrated and centralized, and so many of the most vital sectors of the economy—those directly connected to colonialism—saw the formation of worker's committees, such as the Portuguese airline TAP and the shipyards. These firms were public-private conglomerates directed by the state, so that there was no question of allowing for workers' control as long as the MFA held power. On the other hand, the firms that fell into self-management, where the owners and managers had fled or been expelled, were often barely sustainable economically without hyper-exploitation and state subsidy. Trying to manage output with higher wages and better conditions not only meant they had to produce things differently but sometimes meant they needed to produce entirely different things. The firms which passed into self-management were often the least productive enterprises, who would be undersold in open competition with other producers and so needed to either work harder or be protected from competitive markets. They could appeal to the state for credit or to the movements for solidarity. Unless markets and money were abolished and something else put in their place, capitalist restoration was assured, but within Portugal this was never a real demand. Instead the demand was for autonomy for the workers' councils, but one expressed through their petition for improved conditions. Success would have required a wholesale reorganization of the structure of Portuguese industry, overcoming the division between industry and agriculture in the industrialized south, where large commercial tracts abounded, and small farmers and producers in the conservative, Catholic, and increasingly pro-fascist north, not to mention the boundaries between Portugal and the Spanish economy, itself experiencing a strike wave. As structure the workers' committees could not become the basis for such an effort, and indeed the PRP-BR and LUAR often focused its centralizing energies elsewhere, in the neighborhood assemblies and housing occupations and other place-based bodies, which were in fact more reliably committed to the project of socialization. Even though this was arguably one of the purest expressions of conciliar near-revolution, the locus of action was no longer in the workplace alone. Something had changed, but it would take decades to recognize what.

One way to clarify what had changed is to say that if the revolution of the twentieth century was a circle, centered on the workplace, it was now an ellipse, with one focus eccentric to the workplace and another within it. Self-organization could not be simply the autonomy of the working class itself, for that autonomy divided it from other parts of the proletariat. Nor could it be simply self-organization outside of the workplace, for that would lead to the persistence of capitalist reproduction. It had to emerge both inside and outside the workplace and in the process overcome the distinction between them. It would need to be a geographical, communal body with roots in workplaces but not identical to them, reorganizing reproduction in line with communal and extra-communal need. We might call this body a council or a commune, or perhaps, better, we might come up with a new name. But it would still share something logically with commune and council—it would need to be communist by mandate and rigorously proletarian. It would need to render the reproduction of communism an open book, a living inventory, and allow for everyone to participate in decisions relevant to their life. For the council communists, rooting the delegate structure of the soviets directly in the factories was a way to ensure their proletarian character. Unemployed councils would organize those who could demonstrate proletarian work history. Today perhaps it is this means of proletarianization that would need to be rethought—perhaps Bordiga is correct that the requirement should be dispossession, not exploitation, with the councils open to all those who are "without reserves." Only in this way could such structures become self-reflexive organizations of "the vast majority" in the process of producing real human community—classless, stateless, and moneyless.

These limiting conditions have persisted into the twenty-first century. The cycle of struggles since the economic crisis of 2008 demonstrates what could already be glimpsed in the 1970s—movements emerge eccentric to production, and their passage to insurrection this way tends, leading to a politicization of struggles that are curiously antipolitical in character and therefore unable to follow through on demands, and an orientation toward the state as antagonist or helpmeet. This structure has been perhaps clearest in those insurrections which have involved workers—such as the Oaxacan uprising of 2006, in which a teachers' union led an extended occupation of Oaxaca City in combination with proletarian militants from within and beyond workplaces. In Mexico, where students and teachers frequently hijack buses and interrupt circulation in order to leverage their demands, coming into violent conflict with the state and paramilitary organizations, the eccentricity of struggle to the workplace is quite clear. Another important coordinate is Argentina in 2001, which provides an image of what an insurrectionary mass strike might look like in our time. As the Argentine economy collapsed because of its peg to the US dollar and IMF-led restructuring, antigovernment protests rallying around the antipolitical slogan "Que se vayan todos" forced the resignation of President Fernando de la Rúa. Bank runs and a collapse of the Argentine peso radicalized this movement, allowing for forms of "economic" diffusion that could extend and generalize the insurrectionary political energies of the government-toppling riots of December 2001. Insolvent companies were taken over by workers and put under self-management. *Piqueteros*—groups of unemployed workers who had since the 1990s blocked highways, primarily in rural areas, to demand government aid—collectivized resources, creating networks of free communal provision. Barter networks were established in the cities. But for the most part these forms of expropriation were limited, leaving most of the vast wealth of the Argentine economy untouched. In the big multinational conglomerates, strikes did not turn into occupations. There the economic conditions which were favorable for the takeover of insolvent firms led workers to privilege access to a wage, even a rapidly depreciating one. The isolated firms taken over were saddled with unserviceable debts, and only an appeal to the government for a renegotiation of terms could return them to solvency, a structural dilemma which communization theorists had identified early on, with the 1973 worker takeover of French watchmaker Lip.[27] These were often the least productive firms and required hyperexploitation to earn the average rate of profit. The only alternative was to establish solidarity economies, in exchange with the movement, which would, of course, be contingent upon the movement progressing on other fronts—chiefly, by breaking the armed power of the state.

What would this progress look like? More recent events have not been determinative. Where the armed power of the state has been abnegated it has, as in Portugal, only really been held in abeyance, a process rendered starkly in the Egyptian Revolution and elsewhere during the uprisings of the Arab Spring. What a genuine destruction of the armed power of the state will look like, given modern armies and modern policing, cannot be said in advance, but it can obviously emerge only through a mass demobilization from within, not direct military confrontation. Only history itself can provide a positive form and a positive content, a real communizing process, but in the study so far we have outlined certain logical conditions of this process. It must be proletarian, it must be communist, it must be coordinated by way of revocable mandate, it must be armed and destroy the armed power of the state, and it must overcome divisions between workplace and everyday life, between the economic and the political, not to mention other divisions. These divisions today appear chiefly in the form of the separation of proletarian struggle from production, a separation which movements will have to overcome without affirming an impossible proletarian autonomy within production. Between the lighted focus eccentric to production, and the dimmed focus within it, some diagonal process must emerge, a struggle both inside and outside the workplace.

27 Négation, "Lip and the Self-Managed Counter-revolution," trans. Peter Rachleff and Alan Wallach, *Black and Red* 3 (1975).

All we can see today are precursors of such a process, half-glimpses, past or present, which mostly illuminate the mesh of limits and barriers through which we may surmise the new. In the Portuguese Revolution, many aspects of this new conjuncture could be descried, particularly the problem which the process of conciliar revolution faces when it comes to transnational, globalized capital. A key enterprise in the revolution, as already mentioned, was the Portuguese national airline, TAP, which assumed a role in the economy as large as it did chiefly because of the importance of the African colonies. For this reason, COPCON was loath to let the nascent workers' movement impede production there and militarized TAP after a series of strikes. Workers' commissions—proto-councils, perhaps—had formed in order to coordinate the strikes and enforce worker demands on management, but they were quickly dominated by union and party representatives who proposed co-management, essentially using these structures of self-management to subordinate workers to the prerogatives of the state. The response of the workers' committee was to call for general assemblies, involving not just TAP workers but all workers, to discuss the fate of the company, which—given its centrality to the economy and its predication on colonial domination—concerned all Portuguese proletarians, and indeed many dispossessed Africans as well.[28] Such a general assembly was limited in what it could do in the Portuguese case, but perhaps in another conjuncture, an organization like this, both inside and outside the workplace, might succeed where others failed.

Imagine, extrapolating from current trends, an ecological disaster with a death toll similar to a small war. In the aftermath, a riotous movement emerges, demanding the immediate cessation of all fossil fuel production and an expropriation of the resources of fossil fuel companies for environmental mitigation necessary to keep people alive. Workers within these companies are divided, with some willing to strike and others not, but an occupation by displaced disaster migrants, demanding aid, shuts the companies down. In the conflicts that ensue, there is political crisis and a partial collapse of the armed power of the state. The strike spreads to producers within the fossil fuel supply chain, and solidarity networks are established,

---

28 Reeve, *The Development of Workers' Self-Organization*, 24–5.

expropriating other workplaces in order to support the strikers and migrants. Without specifying form or procedure we can still say that whatever socializing process that emerges here would have to take place both inside and outside production, reforming workplaces and the way people live, in part because work and life are put into question by the climate crisis.

Sometimes it looks like this. In face of some new austerity, injustice, crisis, or disaster, a mass movement gathers eccentric to production, impedes circulation, fights with the police, loots and burns. It is a mass strike yet not a strike. It has its ebbs and flows, its centrifugal and centripetal dynamics, spiraling out from the city center into the suburbs or spiraling inward from suburbs to center. It has no formal systematic means of decision-making or accountability, though these tend to emerge on a local, ad hoc basis, ripe for political capture by actors bad or good. Neither is there any sense of common objective, in the absence of which a kind of blank maximalism dominates. The options are to fight harder or not at all. Tactical brilliance abounds in the absence of any strategy.

This is a movement limited on the one side by the cops and on the other by the economy. It cannot penetrate into production; work continues, for the most part, except where mobilizations become so massive as to shut down the economy indirectly. Inasmuch as it becomes revolutionary, it is a political revolution only and a superficial one at that, able to oust this or that hated leader, but unable to alter the economy or the repressive state apparatus, both of which tend to harden in the face of insurrectionary assault. Politicization of the revolutionary movement leads to electoral dead ends, suicidal referenda, or at best the passage of a law which capital will later nullify. The dead weight of the police and behind it the army stands over and against it. This leads often to a kind of inwardness, an emphasis on ethical values anticipatory of communism, a desire to build the new world in the shell of the old, which can't be realized without extension and intensification of the movement, without the appropriation of social wealth.

Absent some new element, this movement will fail, as others have. It will be crushed or wither away, its partisans scattered. What would it require to succeed? History itself will need give birth to self-reflexive revolutionary organization able to draw in the vast majority of society, spanning workplace and home, town and country, old and young, freely and transparently producing for the free, common use of its members. From commune and council we can derive the logic of such organization but not its sufficient historical conditions, its emergence from and as the disaster of capital.

Organize now or wait for an opportune moment? Yes. In the long run, what will have succeeded is as likely to be the patient work of generations as the quick work of ecstatic weeks. Movements of years and movements of months converge during revolutionary days. But in such moments, no question yes or no is asked, and thus the fact of asking is its own answer. The militant minority, the movement of communists, is a transistor, a black box of some function, but it cannot transmit a signal that does not exist. At the same time, its own noise introduces real infidelities, and so transmission is always to some degree clarification. To seek out and amplify what is critical within proletarian practice, that which is cognizant of its own limits and the need to overcome them, this is the unavoidable intermediary task.

What will have worked? It will have to have been example selected from proletarian struggle and refined, clarified by struggle itself—the theory of the communist example gleaned from the theory and practice of Jan Appel is the theory of replicable action, whose proliferation, extension, and intensification would produce communism. The proliferation of the communist measure spreads by way of the communist measure itself and thus does not need to be formulated before the fact. And yet these measures will spread, or not, at rates that have to do with their mediation by existing networks and relations among proletarians. Here is where Appel's catalytic theory of the party remains relevant. Formal or not, the party is that which catalyzes the communist measure—in Appel's case, the council—it is the critical medium of its transmission in and through practice. It emerges as consequence of the clarifying action of the communist measure itself, which finds its pledges even where no formal organization exists, sharpening contradictions everywhere.

To reflect proletarian struggles, its own or others, to amplify them critically, is therefore the first task of theory. Action that matters is conjunct action, which in its meanings shows itself to be aware of action with others, near or far, past, present, and future, and therefore leads to the compounding of action. What matters organizationally are sites that broadcast and amplify the reproduction of struggle. The task is to establish correspondences, networks in which communist resonances can proliferate.

Therefore the first task for the movement of communists is to observe present struggles, their own and those proximate first and foremost, to reflect them critically—which is to say, from the standpoint of communism and its logical contours. Lenin's newspaper-as-party is an organizational cliché, but it rests upon a truism that every communist organization is a medium of communication for action—this is true of the anti-Leninist correspondence committees of the council communist revival as well. The difference is that, in the latter case, these networks are not places simply for the consolidation of a hegemonic leadership but for the critical proliferation of struggle, the clarification of which will reveal communist consensus as it exists. The goal is not to lead a movement or simply to expand it but to facilitate the spread of revolutionary examples chosen by struggle itself.

Inquiry into class struggle is therefore the bailiwick of the ultraleft, as we have come to define it. The best and most intricately observed and analyzed writing on contemporary struggles is often produced by groups influenced in some way by the council communist revival or its critique from the standpoint of communization—from *Endnotes* to *Théorie Communiste*, *Chuang* to *Angry Workers*, from *Insurgent Notes* to Field Notes at the *Brooklyn Rail*—and it is from these projects, and many others, that I derive my clarification and synthesis of the logic of the current era of struggles. Those who abjure any role in leading struggles are often the best at hearing what they have to say without prejudice, projection, or hyperbole. And while these projects are hardly a relay for proletarian action, when movements do emerge they develop media in which similar debates and discussions occur, and similar knowledge is transmitted.

The brief sketch with which I began this chapter might be a description of any number of recent uprisings and social movements: the Estallido Social in Chile, the gilets jaunes in France, the 2020 George Floyd Uprising (GFU) in the US, not to mention many other examples from the last twenty years. In the case of the latter, there has been very little written about the GFU outside of the journals mentioned above, the project *Ill Will* (also loosely ultraleft in orientation), a collection edited by the Vortex Group and published by PM Press (mostly containing articles published in *Ill Will*), and the book *States of Incarceration* by Zhandarka Kurti and Jarrod Shanahan, published by Field Notes.[29] The absence of meaningful reflection on the GFU has much to do with what Idris Robinson has described as its "denial and disarticulation" by the left, some large portion of which remained transfixed by the Bernie Sanders phenomenon and the media vortex of Donald Trump.[30] In a topsy-turvy early pandemic moment of economic and political chaos, with Trump and his networks engaging in hyperbolic and apocalyptic response to the uprising, liberals and the left produced their own conspiratorial constructions, in which the riots were in a few places limited expressions of a justified discontent and elsewhere the action of malfeasant provocateurs and criminal opportunists. For a brief moment, however, other channels flared bright with the revolutionary example, first and foremost the burning of the third precinct police station in Minneapolis. The movement spread through a mimetic (and even "memetic") contagion, a network of proliferating practices which extended through hundreds of US cities in the first few days of the uprising.[31] These were practices both new and old, refinements of an existing repertoire of tactics, spread through semi-private messaging apps, partly open, partly closed.

The first task of any revolution is the disarming of the police and the arming of the proletariat. This process cannot be accomplished overnight, as we've seen. Even the complete collapse of the German empire and its army in 1918 did not fully abolish the armed power of the state—the conservative officers of the Reich, and their reformed units, competed with the councils and the workers' militias for

29 Vortex Group, ed., *The George Floyd Uprising* (Oakland: PM Press, 2023); Zhandarka Kurti and Jarrod Shanahan, *States of Incarceration: Rebellion, Reform, and America's Punishment System*, Field Notes Series (London: Reaktion Books, 2022).

30 Idris Robinson, "How It Might Should Be Done," *Ill Will*, August 16, 2020, illwill.com.

31 Adrian Wohlleben, "Memes Without End," *Ill Will*, May 16, 2021, illwill.com.

control. We saw glimpses of this collapse of armed state power during the George Floyd Uprising. The spread of the movement from Minneapolis was in part catalyzed by the revolutionary example of the third precinct set on fire—here was a replicable action, both rallying cry and the thing itself, an act which called for more acts, for its insurrectionary reproduction. The destruction of the third precinct was, in part, the result of a tactical retreat by the police, a demobilization not outright defeat, after the precinct was besieged by a combination of armed and nonviolent protestors. Here, too, we saw the replication of new "frontliner tactics," in part learned from the Hong Kong uprising of 2018—the tactical use of lasers, umbrellas, and fireworks to combat and defend oneself from the police.

The movement was characterized, however, by the inability of this action to spread. In early June, in Seattle, where crowds were particularly focused on fighting with the police, skirmishes in front of the police station in the liberal Capitol Hill district led to a similar demobilization, as officers retreated from the building. Some present wanted to burn this police station, too, and attempted to do so, but were restrained by the informal militia present, who were there ostensibly to defend against attacks from MAGA and neo-fascist counter-protestors but in this instance were policing the movement. The decision was instead made to occupy, barricade, and defend the area, now a police-free autonomous zone. Here was another potentially replicable form selected by struggle itself, the autonomous zone, and such zones had already formed in Minneapolis at the site where George Floyd was murdered and would form in other areas as well, as informal loci for the movement. For example, after the police murder of Rayshard Brooks at a Wendy's in Atlanta later in the summer, abolitionist crowds surrounded the fast-food restaurant, burned it, and established an autonomous zone there. That these two revolutionary examples—burning and occupying—were at odds in Seattle, when it is clear that destroying police power and establishing police-free zones are complementary activities, even perhaps activities that presuppose each other, indicates the incoherence of the movement and its undefined goals.

While the burning of police stations did not spread through US cities, arson itself did. One of the first conclusions of an inquiry into the GFU is that fire is enormously effective in rendering American cities ungovernable. Fire demobilizes the police, a pattern repeated in city after city. Once a certain number of fires occur, police shift to passive protection of firefighters, traffic control, and the defense of key sites. This establishes open hunting season on private property, as inchoate looting in the city centers, near sites of confrontation, becomes increasingly organized, brazen, and extensive, with new and existing networks choosing different, poorly guarded targets, usually suburban shopping malls, at an increasing radius from the city center, and conducted with vehicles rather than on foot. In many cities this police holiday lasted for three to five nights, after which point a natural slowdown in looting and arson allowed the police to reestablish control. If they could not, the National Guard would be called in, as happened to some degree in over thirty-one states. By early June, eighty cities were under curfew orders.

This was the critical moment for the movement. Further insurrectionary escalation was blocked, except where organized factions could push things forward, as happened in Portland, leading to a unique sequence of struggle there, or where subsequent local events, such as the Rayshard Brooks murder, reignited a local sequence. Fire was the medium of this movement in its early days but also serves as potent metaphor for its internal dynamic. Fire is uncontrollable and directed by physical variables not knowable in advance, but it also erodes its own conditions for reproduction—it burns out, like riots burn out, leaving itself without air or fuel. For Luxemburg, we will remember, this is the central character of movements, their periodic rhythm, and such a moment might be the precursor for later intensification if this pause allows for its spread to new, fresher material, carrying embers into the haystacks of the town. Something like this did occur, a capillarial proliferation of the movement and its slogans and watchwords in early June and leading up to the historically resonant holidays of Juneteenth and July Fourth, but these did not become the basis for a later re-intensification of the movement. One could no doubt fill a small library with the well-meaning but empty abolitionist legislation proposed during those first weeks, then neutered, the opportunist declarations of opposition to antiblack racism and police violence by organizations, corporations, municipalities, and everyone with a platform, to be forgotten at the first chance.

As the looting dispersed and became more technically complex, it also became less communist, festive, and collective, increasingly monopolized by criminal rackets which would extend their insurrectionary enterprises into the summer and beyond, focusing on high-value targets. After a few weeks of big demonstrations and marches called by liberal groups, the movement became increasingly dominated by militants looking for ways to extend the confrontation. In Portland, where ritual antipolice marches continued nightly throughout June, engaging in continuous skirmishes with the police around the federal building, Trump federalized the police response, effectively creating a new political locus for the movement in Trump. This was what allowed the movement to extend itself into July, as Trump had effectively turned the uprising into a referendum on national history and the unfinished work of Black Reconstruction, made especially clear in the wave of activist removals of Confederate statues, often performed preemptively by the authorities. These topplings extended beyond the Confederates, however, targeting genocidal Reconstructionists as well, and became a way for the movement to articulate its values by way of American history.

Otherwise the movement seemed to struggle to know itself or be known—a paranoid epistemology attended it from the beginning. Who was it? The multiracial character of the uprising, especially of its youth participants, was treated as a scandal, to be explained as police provocation or white-supremacist infiltration. While the right-wing media treated it as a Democrat-led insurrection, the liberal media condoned the riots as justifiable outrage, downplaying their scope and violence, and pointing to the large peaceful daytime marches that came after the insurrectionary days as the real heart of the movement. In the autonomous zones, where coordination and extension might have occurred, the practical problems of police abolition made this impossible. These were effectively lawless zones, which made them areas of opportunity for people of all sorts. Chaotic gunbattles occurred, and people were shot by the movement's defenders, who were clearly neither police nor fascist vigilantes. This is not to say that these autonomous zones could not have been stabilized and extended, but this would have required the establishment of an ethical and organizational consistency rendering them spaces worth fighting for—they would need to be free of the police, but also spaces of real freedom and autonomy for people. In Minneapolis, this did occur to a degree in the early days. A squatted hotel was opened, and people housed for free. Depots were created where looted goods were distributed, but such ventures would have needed to be extended, deepened, and given replicable consistency. Here inquiry must become speculative.

Everyone hates the police, but no one knows what to do about them. The accomplishment of the George Floyd Uprising was its revelation of this fundamental unanimity, which even liberals might admit. Even the police hate the police. The name this unanimity was given by the movement was "abolition"—*abolish the police!* This was its cry, and the burning of the third precinct its objective correlative. But it is impossible to imagine the abolition of the police independent of the abolition of class society, the inauguration of communism. To burn two, three, four, many police stations seems suicidal absent the possibility of cultivating a form of life that could do without the police. Nor can one build the new world in the burnt-out husks of the former—one needs its wealth, its real resources and capabilities. Thus abolition comes to mean everything and nothing. Because the police are an absolute enemy, an absolute bad, one can treat the struggle with them as zero-sum. Any reduction in prison is good. Any reduction in police violence is good, and thus all reforms are abolitionist. But this becomes true, also, of anything that practically improves people's lives.

And yet one must work with the terms which the proletariat has already chosen, as Jan Appel shows us, and in the case of the GFU this is clear. The name of the revolutionary example is "abolition," but it has not yet found its form, whether arson or autonomous zone or something else. Abolition was the name for the soviet without councils of the movement and its revolutionary partisans. And as with the soviets, its meaning was undetermined—it needed a restriction of its participants, a delimitation of its functions. This is how calls for black leadership of the movement could have been answered, not simply by persons but in the fundamental commitment of the movement to abolition, not just the overcoming of the police but the long history of racial domination in the US, the unfinished work of the abolition of slavery—which is to say, the abolition of class society and, with it, racialization. What if, in Minneapolis or somewhere else, in these early days, a vast abolition assembly were held, the result of which was the formation of an abolition committee and the permanent occupation of a given space? What if this spread to other cities? What if these committees could wax and wane as the movement went through its phases, extending the energies of some initial moment into a subsequent insurrectionary heightening? These would be spaces where the meaning of abolition would have to be determined practically, both through the production of zones free from policing and through a practical overcoming of the structures of antiblack racism, both internal and external. This would naturally involve the leadership and participation of black proletarians, but just as importantly the leadership and participation of those fundamentally committed to abolition, in all its disclosed meanings.

The abolition committee in my construction is a heuristic fiction, a placeholder, a name for a form that has not emerged. It should not be taken literally, and such a form can become answer only to questions posed by movements themselves—they emerge by necessity and not by choice, and as expression of the proletarian, communist content of such a movement. To call for committees or councils absent such a moment is to shout into the void. Nonetheless, this fiction is useful in probing certain functions that would need to be accomplished if the movement were to succeed in becoming revolutionary, and obviously requires a great deal of abstraction from the particular issues of the GFU. What would these abolition committees need to do, other than abolish class society and with it the proletariat and themselves? First and foremost they would need to serve as critical reflector and amplifier for the content of struggle itself, for the distribution of viable tactics and forms that might sharpen the movement's means and clarify its ends, extending the energies of the riots into new social categories and spaces. They would need to catalyze action among non-militants and non-activists, in workplaces, schools, prisons. They would need to establish correspondences, through print and other media, and in this way allow for self-reflexivity. They would need to establish open entry points, ways that people can get involved, both in real life and online.

From the beginning we can expect these committees would be dominated by opportunist or at best reformist groups and steered toward legislation and electoral work. A tendency toward the creation of a constitutional amendment or national referendum would likely emerge, as happened with the gilets jaunes in France and the Estallido Social in Chile, and earlier with Podemos in Spain and Syriza in Greece. These tendencies would need to be resisted by the cultivation of organizational capacity outside the milieus typical of the left—such resistance would require the extension of such developments into workplaces and neighborhoods and the cultivation of real capacity for self-organization there, which might resist the politicization of the movement. Coordination must be sought outside the state. Here is where inquiry could become the very form of organization. The abolition committees could engage not only in practical work but in speculative work—*What would abolition look like? What would it require?*

While riots, occupations, blockades, sabotage, and expropriation unfolded, abolition inquiry committees could essentially develop plans for communism. Their founding questions would be: What would you do if state power vanished today? What would you do if there were no more police, and behind them no more army? What would you do if all the prisons burned? A key task for such inquiry committees would be technical inquiry into the conditions of capitalist production and everyday life. The appropriation and transformation of existing means of production into communist production and distribution are also the appropriation and transformation of the knowledge corresponding to such means, their virtual dimension, rendering them transparent and tractable to anyone and everyone. This is a speculative process because the question for communists is not just how *does* this work but how *could* it work. A communist looks at a power plant, a factory, a supermarket, a fleet of buses, or a farm always with an eye to what it could be in communism, which is not at all what it is in capitalism. But what it could be is fundamentally determined by what it is, and therefore knowledge of the database of existing resources is the first step toward producing a real story of communism from them.

What do people do for work where you live? What is produced, using what inputs? Where does the electricity come from? The water? How are the markets supplied? Few of us know the answers to these questions with any depth. For Appel, the role of the communist party was to provide a framework, the councils, which is also to say its theory. The *Grundprinzipien* is a model that can be applied through a deliberative appropriation. But here I think of a framework at a more fundamental level, not a blueprint but a map with the location of the elements from which a blueprint might be constructed by the builders themselves.[32] Less a common plan than a plan for a common plan. The construction of the map would also be in part a work of joining those possessing its constituent knowledge, building connections with people who work for the water department, the power provider, who distribute to the markets. The idea is to imagine an atlas of communist reproduction, with all the knowledge a communist movement might need to begin reproducing itself, at some given insurrectionary juncture. The collection and refinement of such data entirely before the fact is, of course, impossible, but this does not mean nothing can be collected. Any clarification beforehand is likely to help.

These maps can be useful during the mass strike phase of a movement as well, long before the question of communization or socialization of wealth can be raised. During the initial moment of the George Floyd Uprising, when the police were paralyzed by the work of fire suppression, nearly anything that militants wanted to do could have been done, but crowds lacked clear goals or targets. They did not know, aside from a few key landmarks, where the sites of power lay. The distribution of a map with targets, as well as necessary tools, could have gone a long way to catalyzing militant action in this moment. The selection of such targets requires sensitivity to the revolutionary example—one picks targets which the movement is likely to recognize, merely by name or by sight, as valid.

Key here is the work of what I have called "counterlogistics"—mapping capitalist circulation and seeking out its chokepoints, places where a blockade can interrupt production.[33] Ports, airports, logistical hubs, and intermodal exchanges are central here. We live in the era of the protest blockade, a blockade which, when stationary,

32 This notion of map owes something to Fredric Jameson's call for "cognitive maps" in his seminal essay on postmodernism. Fredric Jameson, "Postmodernism, or the Cultural Logic of Late Capitalism," *New Left Review* 146 (July/August 1984): 89–92.

33 Jasper Bernes, "Logistics, Counterlogistics, and the Communist Prospect," *Endnotes* 3 (September 2013): 172–201.

becomes an occupation, a *bloccupation*. Proletarian movements increasingly seek their power over production outside of production, but this is a power that must penetrate to the heart of production. It must interrupt capitalist production, either by winning workers over to its side and convincing them to down their tools or making it impossible for production to continue. Here classical workers' inquiry and the development of base unions or workplace committees is essential—these movements must seek out allies within production. How this happens is one of the essential questions of communist research in our moment.

The weakness of present movements discloses their potential strengths. When proletarians, who may be workers but have no opportunities to intervene in their own workplaces, blockade the workplaces of other proletarians, they reveal the antinomies of self-organization, the need for self-organization to become the with-other-organization of the universal commune. In examining the history of the pre-revolutionary mass strike, we see two deviations from the path of communism—the soviets or councils are declared before proletarians are actively in control of their workplaces; or alternately workers seize their workplaces but without the establishment of coordinative mechanism, forcing them to rely on the state as negotiator, or arbiter, of socialization as nationalization. If the workers organize only for themselves, collectivizing their workplace on their own, disconnected from other expropriations, then they are forced to rely on the market (which will punish them), on volunteerism (which will wane), or the state (which will betray them to the capitalist class). But if they organize only for each other, forming the councils without an intensive basification in workplaces or other centers of proletarian life, then they fail to meaningfully change the conditions of everyday life and lose the chance to incorporate the vast majority in a communist project. The blockaders treat capital from the standpoint of communism, as common property, belonging to everyone and no one. They recognize that capital is a social relation involving everyone, the proletariat first and foremost, in the project of the common destruction of class society by a vastly proletarian humanity. If a factory is manufacturing weapons used to kill you, it is not merely the concerns of its workers. But, for the workers, those capitals are the means of survival—their ethical claim is real, though pertinent only to capital. If you keep them from work and bankrupt their company, they will starve absent other means to reproduce themselves.

Solutions to this dilemma can emerge only through antagonism diagonal to these categories. Since 1968, struggle has emerged eccentric to production, as one focus of an ellipse having its other in the quieted workplace. Only struggle both within and without production can overcome this divide. The name which *Théorie Communiste* has developed for such proto-communist struggle is *l'écart*, which gives to the event the name of the problem it overcomes—the "swerve" between circulation struggle and the missing focus of production which overcomes the "rift" or "gap" between proletarian struggle and its object, sedimented in the distribution of the means of production.[34]

If something like councils were to emerge in the decades to come, it is likely they would not be workers' councils in the strict sense. The ellipse with its two foci would need collapse into the circle of communist reproduction, but this would be the contraction not to the prior center in the workplace but rather to the tangent point of production and circulation, overcoming the division between the two, primarily by delinking social contribution from social distribution at the individual level. The process whereby this will be achieved will require a living inventory of resources and capacities, by no means exhaustive, but sufficient to the needs of provisioning for common use. Communism is an open book whose readers write it freely—the greatest story not yet told.

34 Roland Simon and *Théorie Communiste*, "Théorie de l'écart," *Théorie Communiste* 20 (September 2005); Roland Simon, "The Present Moment," *Sic* 1, no. 1 (November 2011): 96, sicjournal.org.

Acknowledgments

Revolution is a collective affair but writing a solitary one. Dozens of friends and comrades read drafts of this book, contributed to discussions of it, and made vitally important recommendations. Responsibility for the book is nonetheless mine alone. I am enormously grateful to each and every one of these readers, and hope I have told them so personally. My closest readers know who they are. It is, however, important to name collectives and institutions which have contributed to this project. Chapter 2 grew out of independent discussions with the podcast *Reel Abstractions* and a New Institute for Social Research. Red May hosted a discussion of chapter 2 and later, with Ahuehuete, hosted an online lecture series and discussion group through which I developed chapter 1 of this book. Tamarack Oakland provided space for an in-person discussion group, and the Friends of the Classless Society sponsored a talk in Berlin. Finally, I would like to thank my editors at Verso, Ben Mabie and Sebastian Budgen, as well as the entire Verso team, who have turned my manuscript into a book and told people about it.

Index